VOWEL SOUNDS

Symbol	Examples
a	act, bat
ā	day, age
är	air, dare
ä	father, star
e	edge, ten
ē	speed, money
ə*	ago, system, easily, compete, focus
ēr	dear, pier
i	fit, is
ī	sky, bite
o	not, wasp
ō	nose, over
ô	law, order
oi	noise, enjoy
ōō	true, boot
oo	put, look
yōō	cute, united
ou	loud, cow
u	fun, up
ûr	learn, urge, butter, word

*This symbol, the schwa, represents the sound of unaccented vowels. It sounds like "uh."

CONSONANT SOUNDS

Symbol	Examples
b	back, cab
ch	cheap, match, picture
d	door, head
f	fan, leaf, phone
g	give, dog
h	her, behave
j	just, page
k	king, bake, car
l	leaf, roll
m	my, home
n	note, rain
ng	sing, bank
p	put, stop
r	red, far
s	say, pass
sh	ship, push
t	to, let
th	thin, with
TH	THat, baTHe
v	value, live
w	want, away
y	yes, onion
z	zoo, maze, rise
zh	pleasure, vision

Why Do You Need this New Edition?

If you're wondering why you should buy this new edition of *Academic Vocabulary*, here are eight good reasons!

1. Twenty-three new vocabulary words for you to master and apply to your everyday life.

2. Seven new or expanded engaging readings for you to practice and apply your vocabulary skills.

3. Two additional Review Chapters for you to test your mastery of the vocabulary words.

4. Two new collaborative activities in the Review Chapters, titled "Mix It Up," so that you can work with your classmates to develop your vocabulary skills.

5. New "Conversation Starters" and "Word Part Reminders" to help you become familiar with key terms.

6. The analogy Self-Tests have been moved to the latter part of a chapter to allow you more time to work with the vocabulary words before encountering this challenging activity.

7. A Glossary has been added for easy reference to the vocabulary words.

8. A new Web site has been developed for additional practice, replacing the CD-ROM.

Academic Vocabulary

Academic Words

Fourth Edition

Amy E. Olsen
Cuesta College

Longman

New York   San Francisco   Boston
London   Toronto   Sydney   Tokyo   Singapore   Madrid
Mexico City   Munich   Paris   Cape Town   Hong Kong   Montreal

Dedication

To Dr. Stockmann and Miss H.

Thanks for sticking around. The same goes for the wonderful characters I've had the pleasure of encountering in person and in literature.

—AMY E. OLSEN

Acquisitions Editor: Kate Edwards
Marketing Manager: Thomas DeMarco
Senior Supplements Editor: Donna Campion
Senior Media Producer: Stefanie Liebman
Production Manager: Savoula Amanatidis
Project Coordination, Text Design, and Electronic Page Makeup: Elm Street Publishing Services
Cover Design Manager: Wendy Ann Fredericks
Cover Designer: Nancy Sacks
Cover Photos: Bottom left by Katy Tallorin; all others by Amy E. Olsen
Photo Researcher: Linda Sykes
Senior Manufacturing Buyer: Dennis J. Para
Printer and Binder: Quad/Graphics—Dubuque
Cover Printer: Lehigh-Phoenix Color Corporation

Photo Credits: **p. 8 (T):** Hulton Archive/Getty Images; **p. 8 (B):** Mark Richards/PhotoEdit, Inc.; **p. 14:** Amy E. Olsen; **p. 22:** Dan A. Tallorin; **p. 26 (T):** David Weintraub/Photo Researchers, Inc.; **p. 26 (M):** Amy E. Olsen; **p. 26 (B):** John Serrao/Photo Researchers, Inc.; **p. 29:** Tony Olsen; **p. 34:** Amy E. Olsen; **p. 40:** Amy E. Olsen; **p. 43:** Amy E. Olsen; **p. 44 (T):** © Artiga Photo/Corbis; **p. 44 (B):** Charles Gupton/Stone/Getty Images; **p. 46:** David Young-Wolff/PhotoEdit, Inc.; **p. 50 (T):** Tham/The Image Works; **p. 50 (M):** Express/Getty Images; **p. 50 (B):** Chris Moorhouse; **p. 56 (T):** Amy E. Olsen; **p. 56 (B):** Jeff Greenberg/PhotoEdit, Inc.; **p. 58:** Amy E. Olsen; **p. 60:** Tony Olsen; **p. 62 (T):** BP, NRSC/Photo Researchers, Inc.; **p. 62 (B):** Amy E. Olsen; **p. 64:** Amy E. Olsen; **p. 65:** Milt Olsen; **p. 66:** Amy E. Olsen; **p. 70:** Katy Tallorin; **p. 76:** Amy E. Olsen; **p. 80 (L):** Amy E. Olsen; **p. 80 (R):** Amy E. Olsen; **p. 82:** Amy E. Olsen; **p. 84:** Amy E. Olsen; **p. 86:** David Young-Wolff/PhotoEdit, Inc.; **p. 88:** Amy E. Olsen; **p. 92 (L):** The Everett Collection; **p. 92 (R):** The Everett Collection; **p. 95:** Amy E. Olsen; **p. 98 (T):** Will and Demi McIntyre/Photo Researchers, Inc.; **p. 98 (B):** Jim Drivas Photography; **p. 101:** Jeff Greenberg/PhotoEdit, Inc.; **p. 106:** Amy E. Olsen; **p. 112:** Milt Olsen; **p. 116 (T):** Spencer Arnold/Getty Images; **p. 116 (B):** AKG/Photo Researchers, Inc.; **p. 122:** Amy E. Olsen; **p. 125:** Amy E. Olsen; **p. 126 (T):** Amy E. Olsen; **p. 126 (B):** Amy E. Olsen; **p. 128:** Amy E. Olsen; **p. 129:** Amy E. Olsen; **p. 134 (T):** David Hosking/Frank Lane Pictures/Photo Researchers, Inc.; **p. 134 (B):** Milt Olsen; **p. 136:** Milt Olsen; **p. 137:** Tham/The Image Works; **p. 138:** Amy E. Olsen; **p. 142:** Amy E. Olsen; **p. 145:** Amy E. Olsen; **p. 146 (T):** Flying Colours Ltd./Digital Vision/Getty Images RF; **p. 146 (B):** Scott T. Baxter/Photodisc/Getty Images RF; **p. 149:** Gerald Warnken Jr.; **p. 152 (T):** Pushkin Museum of Fine Arts, Moscow. Copyright Scala/Art Resource, NY; **p. 152 (B):** National Gallery, London, UK. Copyright Erich Lessing/Art Resource, NY; **p. 153:** Neil Emmerson/Robert Harding Imagery/Corbis; **p. 154:** Collection of the Newark Museum, Newark, New Jersey. Copyright The Newark Museum/Art Resource, NY. © 2002 The Georgia O'Keeffe Foundation/Artists Rights Society (ARS), New York; **p. 155:** Katy Tallorin; **p. 156:** Digital Image © The Museum of Modern Art/Licensed by SCALA/Art Resource, NY. © Estate of Pablo Picasso, Artists Rights Society (ARS), NY; **p. 158:** Ricky John Mallor/Taxi/Getty Images; **p. 162 (T):** Amy E. Olsen; **p. 162 (B):** Amy E. Olsen; **p. 164 (T):** Eric Meola/The Image Bank/Getty Images; **p. 164 (B):** Amy E. Olsen; **p. 172:** Amy E. Olsen.

Longman
is an imprint of

www.pearsonhighered.com

ISBN-13: 978-0-205-63318-0
ISBN-10:   0-205-63318-8

3 4 5 6 7 8 9 10—V042—12 11

Contents

Preface

Because students benefit greatly from increased word power, the study of vocabulary should be enjoyable. Unfortunately, vocabulary workbooks often lose sight of this goal. To make the study of vocabulary an exciting and enjoyable part of college study, I wrote *Academic Vocabulary*.

The goal of this book—the third in a three-book interactive vocabulary series—is to make the study of vocabulary fun through a variety of thematic readings, self-tests, and interactive exercises. As a casual glimpse through the book will indicate, these activities involve writing, personal experience, art, and many other formats. The goal of these activities is simple: to utilize individual learning styles in order to help students learn new words in a large number of contexts.

Underlying the text's strong visual appeal is the philosophy that an essential part of learning vocabulary is repeated exposure to a word. *Academic Vocabulary* provides eight exposures to each vocabulary word in the text plus more opportunities for exposure through the Collaborative Activities and games in the Instructor's Manual.

Content Overview

Academic Vocabulary is an ideal text for both classroom and self-study. The twenty main chapters follow a consistent format.

- **Thematic Reading:** Because most vocabulary is acquired through reading, each chapter—with the exception of the Word Parts and Review Chapters—begins with a thematic reading that introduces ten vocabulary words in context. These readings come in a variety of formats, from worksheets to essays. The goal is to show that new words may be encountered anywhere. Rather than simply presenting a word list with definitions, students have the opportunity to discover the meanings of these new words via context clues.

    The themes for *Academic Vocabulary* were chosen from disciplines that most students will encounter at some point in their college careers. In choosing the words, I've been guided by five factors: (1) relation to the chapter theme; (2) use in textbooks, novels, magazines, and newspapers; (3) occurrence in standardized tests such as the SAT and GRE; (4) containing word parts introduced in the text; and (5) my own experiences in teaching reading and writing.
- **Predicting:** The second page of each chapter contains a Predicting activity that gives students the chance to figure out the meaning of each vocabulary word before looking at its definition. The Predicting section helps students learn the value of context clues in determining a word's meaning. While the text does offer information on dictionary use, I strongly advocate the use of context clues as one of the most active methods of vocabulary development.
- **Self-Tests:** Following the Predicting activity are three Self-Tests in various formats. With these tests, students can monitor their comprehension. The tests include text and sentence completion, true/false situations, matching, and analogies. Some tests employ context clue strategies such as synonyms and antonyms and general meaning. Critical thinking skills are an important part of each test. (Answers to the Self-Tests appear in the Instructor's Manual.)
- **Word Wise:** Following the Self-Tests is the Word Wise section that teaches a variety of skills that are helpful to vocabulary acquisition. There are seven types of activities: Internet Activities, A Different Approach, Context Clue Mini-Lessons, Interesting Etymologies, Collocations, Word Pairs, and Connotations and Denotations. Each activity is explained in the Getting Started section. These activities give students additional practice and insight into the words they are learning.

- **Interactive Exercise:** Next is an Interactive Exercise that may include writing, making lists, or answering questions. The Interactive Exercises give students the chance to really think about the meanings of the words, but, more importantly, they encourage students to begin using the words actively. Some instructors have their students do the Interactive Exercise in small groups (or pairs) and then have the groups share their responses with the whole class. (See the Instructor's Manual for more collaborative activities.)
- **Hint, Word Part Reminder, or Conversation Starters:** Each chapter includes a Hint, a Word Part Reminder, or Conversation Starters. The Hints cover tips for developing vocabulary, reading, or study skills; they are brief and practical, and students will be able to make use of them in all of their college courses. The Word Part Reminders are short exercises that give students a chance to practice using a few of the word parts they have recently learned. The Conversation Starters are questions that ask students to use the words while speaking with each other. The goal of the Conversation Starters is to get students to use the words in daily life.
- **Word List:** The last page in a chapter contains a list of the vocabulary words with a pronunciation guide, the part of speech, and a brief definition. I wrote these definitions with the idea of keeping them simple and nontechnical. Some vocabulary texts provide complicated dictionary definitions that include words students do not know; I've tried to make the definitions as friendly and as useful as possible.
- **Words to Watch:** The final activity asks students to pick three to five words they may be having trouble with and to write their own sentences using the words. This section is an additional chance for students to grasp the meaning of a few words that may be difficult for them.

Additional Features

In addition to the thematic vocabulary chapters, *Academic Vocabulary* includes the following sections to assist students in learning new vocabulary.

- **Getting Started:** The text begins with an introductory chapter to familiarize students with some of the tools of vocabulary acquisition. The "Parts of Speech" section gives sample words and sentences for the eight parts of speech. "Using the Dictionary" dissects a sample dictionary entry and provides an exercise for using guide words. "Completing Analogies" explains how analogies work, provides sample analogies, and gives students analogy exercises to complete. This section will prepare students for the analogy Self-Tests contained in several chapters of the text. The "Benefits of Flash Cards" section explains the advantages of using flash cards and encourages students to make flash cards beginning with Chapter 1. The "Word Wise Features" section provides background information for the various Word Wise activities.
- **Word Parts:** The three Word Parts chapters introduce prefixes, roots, and suffixes used throughout the book. Students learn the meanings of these forms, and sample words illustrate the forms. Self-Tests in each Word Parts chapter give students the opportunity to practice using the word parts.
- **Review Chapters:** Five Review Chapters focus on the preceding four chapters. They divide the words into different activity groups and test students' cumulative knowledge. The words appear in artistic, test, written, puzzle, and collaborative formats. These repeated and varied exposures increase the likelihood that students will remember the words, not just for one chapter or test, but for life.
- **Glossary:** The Glossary is new to this edition. It lists all the vocabulary words along with the part of speech and the definitions given in each chapter. Students may find it handy to refer to the Glossary when reviewing words from several chapters.
- **Create Your Own Flash Cards:** The "Create Your Own Flash Cards" section teaches students how to make and use flash cards. Students can use the cards for self-study. Additionally, instructors can use them for the supplemental activities and games found in the Instructor's Manual.

- **Pronunciation Key:** On the inside front cover is a pronunciation key to help students understand the pronunciation symbols used in this text. The inside front cover also offers some additional guidelines on pronunciation issues.
- **Word List:** The inside back cover features a list of all the vocabulary words and the page numbers on which the definitions are given. A list of the word parts from the Word Parts chapters is also included on the inside back cover with page references.

Features New to this Edition

This fourth edition has several new features in response to instructor comments.

- **Refined Chapter Organization:** The chapters have been rearranged to start with what can be considered core classes: social science (U. S. history), composition, mathematics, and physical science (biology). The rest of the text contains more social science, arts and humanities, and physical science courses, as well as chapters covering courses found in business, technology, and education departments. This organizational method is designed to address the needs of most students at the start of the text, and then to keep student interest high by presenting a variety of disciplines in each section.
- **Refined In-Chapter Organization:** All of the analogy Self-Tests have been moved to the third exercise in a chapter to allow students more time to work with the vocabulary words before encountering this challenging activity.
- **Added Content:** Two additional Review Chapters have been added to help students reinforce and more quickly assess their learning of the words. Word Part Reminders and Conversation Starters have been interspersed with the Hints as additional ways to help students remember the word parts and vocabulary words. A Glossary has been added to aid instructors and students in quickly finding a definition they want to review.
- **New Readings:** About a third of the chapters have new readings in either topics or formats more likely to appeal to students. Some of the chapters have also been lengthened to give students more reading practice and to increase a student's cultural literacy about a topic. Additionally, new words have been added to some chapters.
- **Updated Design:** New photographs have been added to several chapters to make the text more visually friendly. The artwork has been redone in some chapters for a more sophisticated look. And the layout of the text has been redesigned for simplicity and freshness.
- **New Web Site:** The CD-ROM that formerly accompanied *Academic Vocabulary* has been transferred to the Internet to allow for easier student access and timelier updating of the exercises.

The Teaching and Learning Package

Each component of the teaching and learning package for *Academic Vocabulary* has been carefully crafted to maximize the main text's value.

- **Instructor's Manual and Test Bank (ISBN: 0-205-63326-9):** The Instructor's Manual and Test Bank includes options for additional Collaborative Activities and games. The collaborative section explains ways students can share their work on the Interactive Exercises in pairs, in small groups, or with the whole class. Ideas for other collaborative activities using different learning styles are also offered. The games section presents games that can be used with individual chapters or for review of several chapters. The games include both individual and full-class activities. The Collaborative Activities and games give students the opportunity to use the words in conversational settings and a chance to work with others.

  The Test Bank, formatted for easy copying, includes two tests for each chapter and combined tests of two chapters. Mastery Tests accompany the Review Chapters and full-book Mastery Tests can be used as final exams.
- *Academic Vocabulary* **Web Site:** Available with this text is access to the *Academic Vocabulary* Web site, which features additional exercises and tests that provide for more interaction between the students and the words. The Web site has an audio component that allows students

to hear each chapter's thematic reading and the pronunciation of each word as often as they choose. Students are often reluctant to use the new words they learn because they aren't sure how to pronounce them. The pronunciation guides in each chapter do help to address this fear, but actually hearing the words spoken will give students greater confidence in using the words. To learn how to access the Web site, contact your Pearson publishing representative.

For Additional Reading and Reference

The Longman Basic Skills Package

In addition to the book-specific supplements discussed above, other skills-based supplements are available. These supplements are available either at no additional cost or at greatly reduced prices.

- **The Dictionary Deal.** Two dictionaries can be shrink-wrapped with *Academic Vocabulary* at a nominal fee. *The New American Webster Handy College Dictionary* is a paperback reference text with more than 100,000 entries. *Merriam-Webster's Collegiate Dictionary,* Eleventh Edition, is a hardback reference with a citation file of more than 14.5 million examples of English words drawn from actual use. For more information, please contact your Pearson publishing representative.
- **Longman Vocabulary Web Site.** For additional vocabulary-related resources, visit our free vocabulary Web site at http://www.ablongman.com/vocabulary.
- **MyReadingLab (www.myreadinglab.com).** MyReadingLab is the first and only online learning system to diagnose both students' reading skills and reading levels. This remarkable program utilizes diagnostic testing, personalized practice, and gradebook reports to allow instructors to measure student performance and help students gain control over their reading.

Acknowledgments

I want to thank the following reviewers for their helpful suggestions for this fourth edition: Cecelia Guinee, Portland Community College; Kimberly Smith, Miami Dade College–Homestead Campus; Cynthia Graham, Pueblo Community College; Carol Horner, John Tyler Community College; Marianne Friedell, College of the Mainland; Nancy Banks, Florida Community College of Jacksonville; Judy Johnson, John Tyler Community College; and Keming Liu, Medgar Evers College/CUNY.

Additionally, I am grateful to Kate Edwards, Acquisitions Editor of Reading and Study Skills at Pearson Longman for her help in preparing this edition. Commendations go to Pearson's Supplement and Marketing departments for their assistance and to Elm Street Publishing Services for making this series visually appealing. A big thank you to Martha Beyerlein for her work during the production phase. To Elizabeth, Tina, and Margaret, as well as other colleagues, I offer my gratitude for stimulating discussions on education at various gatherings. I deeply appreciate my family's support, and I give warm thanks to my husband for being such a good guy.

I am proud to present the fourth edition of *Academic Vocabulary,* a book that makes learning vocabulary enjoyable and meaningful.

—AMY E. OLSEN

Also Available

Books 1 and 2 of the Vocabulary Series:
  Interactive Vocabulary: General Words, by Amy E. Olsen
  Active Vocabulary: General and Academic Words, by Amy E. Olsen

Getting Started

Parts of Speech

There are eight parts of speech. A word's part of speech is based on how the word is used in a sentence. Words can, therefore, be more than one part of speech. For an example, note how the word *punch* is used below.

nouns: (n.) name a person, place, or thing

> EXAMPLES: Ms. Lopez, New Orleans, lamp, warmth
>
> *Ms. Lopez* enjoyed her *trip* to *New Orleans* where she bought a beautiful *lamp*. The *warmth* of the *sun* filled *Claire* with *happiness*. I drank five *cups* of the orange *punch*.

pronouns: (pron.) take the place of a noun

> EXAMPLES: I, me, you, she, he, it, her, we, they, my, which, that, anybody, everybody
>
> *Everybody* liked the music at the party. *It* was the kind that made people want to dance. *They* bought a new car, *which* hurt their bank account.

verbs: (v.) express an action or state of being

> EXAMPLES: enjoy, run, think, read, dance, am, is, are, was, were
>
> Lily *read* an interesting book yesterday. I *am* tired. He *is* an excellent student. She *punched* the bully.

adjectives: (adj.) modify (describe or explain) a noun or pronoun

> EXAMPLES: pretty, old, two, expensive, red, small
>
> The *old* car was covered with *red* paint on *one* side. The *two* women met for lunch at an *expensive* restaurant. The *punch* bowl was *empty* soon after Uncle Al got to the party.

adverbs: (adv.) modify a verb, an adjective, or another adverb

> EXAMPLES: very, shortly, first, too, soon, quickly, finally, furthermore, however
>
> We will meet *shortly* after one o'clock. The *very* pretty dress sold *quickly*. I liked her; *however,* there was something strange about her.

prepositions: (prep.) are placed before a noun or pronoun to create a phrase that relates to other parts of the sentence

> EXAMPLES: after, around, at, before, by, from, in, into, of, off, on, through, to, up, with
>
> He told me to be *at* his house *in* the afternoon. You must go *through* all the steps to do the job.

conjunctions: (conj.) join words or other sentence elements and show a relationship between the connected items

> EXAMPLES: and, but, or, nor, for, so, yet, after, although, because, if, since, than, when
>
> I went to the movies, *and* I went to dinner on Tuesday. I will not go to the party this weekend *because* I have to study. I don't want to hear your reasons *or* excuses.

interjections: (interj.) show surprise or emotion

> EXAMPLES: oh, hey, wow, ah, ouch
>
> *Oh,* I forgot to do my homework! *Wow,* I got an A on the test!

Using the Dictionary

There will be times when you need to use a dictionary for one of its many features; becoming familiar with dictionary **entries** will make using a dictionary more enjoyable. The words in a dictionary are arranged alphabetically. The words on a given page are signaled by **guide words** at the top of the page. If the word you are looking for comes alphabetically between these two words, then your word is on that page. When using online dictionaries, you will simply type in the word you are looking for, so guide words will not be important, but the other features of an entry remain the same.

1436   **wing tip • wintry** ← Guide words

← Entry

wing tip *n* (ca. 1908) **1a** : the edge or outer margin of a bird's wing **b** *usu* **wingtip** : the outer end of an airplane wing **2** : a toe cap having a point that extends back toward the throat of the shoe and curving sides that extend toward the shank **3** : a shoe having a wing tip

¹**wink**\ˈwiŋk\ *vb* [ME, fr. OE *wincian*; akin to OHG *winchan* to stagger, wink and perh. to L *vacillare* to sway, Skt *vāncati* he goes crookedly] *vi* (bef. 12c) **1** : to shut one eye briefly as a signal or in teasing **2** : to close and open the eyelids quickly **3** : to avoid seeing or noting something — usu. used with *at* **4** : to gleam or flash intermittently: TWINKLE <her glasses ~*ing* in the sunlight — Harper Lee> **5 a** : to come to an end — usu. used with *out* **b** : to stop shining — usu. used with *out* **6** : to signal a message with a light ~ *vt* **1** : to cause to open and shut **2** : to affect or influence by or as if by blinking the eyes

²**wink** *n* (14c) **1** : a brief period of sleep : NAP <catching a ~> **2 a** : a hint or sign given by winking **b** : an act of winking **3** : the time of a wink: INSTANT <quick as a ~> **4** : a flicker of the eyelids: BLINK

win·ter·ize \ˈwin-tə-ˌrīz\ *vt* **-ized** ; **-iz·ing** (1934) : to make ready for winter or winter use and esp. resistant or proof against winter weather <~ a car> — **win·ter·i·za·tion** \ˌwin-tə-rə-ˈzā-shən\ *n*

win·ter—kill \ˈwin-tər-ˌkil\ *vt* (ca. 1806) : to kill (as a plant) by exposure to winter conditions ~ *vi* : to die as a result of exposure to winter conditions — **winterkill** *n*

win·ter·ly \ˈwin-tər-lē\ *adj* (1559) : of, relating to, or occurring in winter : WINTRY

winter melon *n* (ca. 1900) **1** : any of several muskmelons (as a casaba or honeydew melon) that are fruits of a cultivated vine (*Cucumis melo indorus*) **2** : a large white-fleshed melon that is the fruit of an Asian vine (*Benincasa hispida*) and is used esp. in Chinese cooking

winter quarters *n pl but sing or pl in constr* (1641) : a winter residence or station (as of a military unit or a circus)

winter savory *n* (1597) : a perennial European mint (*Satureja montana*) with leaves used for seasoning — compare SUMMER SAVORY

winter squash *n* (1775) : any of various hard-shelled squashes that belong to cultivars

SOURCE: By permission. From *Merriam-Webster's Collegiate® Dictionary*, Eleventh Edition © 2008 by Merriam-Webster, Incorporated (www.Merriam-Webster.com).

Using Guide Words

Use the sample guide words to determine on which page each of the eight words will be found. Write the page number next to the entry word.

Page	Guide Words
157	bone/boo
159	boot/born
654	humanist/humongous
655	humor/hunter
975	pamphlet/pandemonium
976	pander/pant

EXAMPLE: _654_ humdinger

_____ 1. pang

_____ 2. Panama

_____ 3. bonnet

_____ 4. hummus

_____ 5. border

_____ 6. hunk

_____ 7. booth

_____ 8. pansy

Most dictionaries contain the following information in an entry:

- The **pronunciation**—symbols that show how a word should be spoken, including how the word is divided into syllables and where the stress should be placed on a word. The Pronunciation Key for this book is located on the inside front cover. The key shows the symbols used to indicate the sound of a word. Every dictionary has a pronunciation method, and a pronunciation key or guide is usually found in the front pages, with a partial key at the bottom of each page. The differences in the pronunciation systems used by dictionaries are usually slight.
- The **part of speech**—usually abbreviated, such as *n.* for noun, *v.* for verb, and *adj.* for adjective. A key to these abbreviations and others is usually found in the front of the dictionary.
- The **definition**—usually the most common meaning is listed first followed by other meanings.
- An **example of the word in a sentence**—the sentence is usually in italics and follows each meaning.
- **Synonyms** and **antonyms**—*synonyms* are words with similar meanings, and *antonyms* are words with opposite meanings. (You should also consider owning a **thesaurus,** a book that lists synonyms and antonyms.)
- The **etymology**—the history of a word, usually including the language(s) it came from.
- The **spelling of different forms** of the word—these forms may include unusual plurals and verb tenses (especially irregular forms).

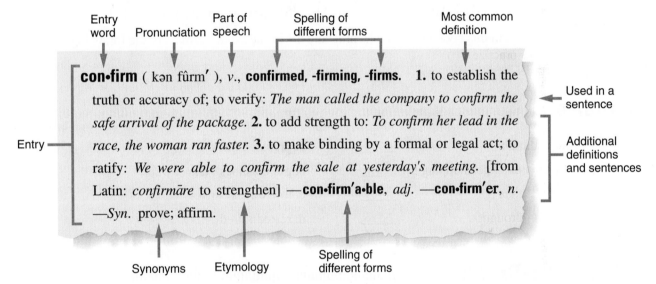

Despite the popularity of online dictionaries, it can still be handy to own a paper version. When choosing a dictionary, take the time to look at different dictionaries to see what appeals to you. Dictionaries come in several sizes and are made for different purposes. First read some of the entries to see if the definitions make sense to you. See which of the features above are used in the dictionary. Is it important to you to be able to study the etymology of a word? Would you like sample sentences? Some dictionaries have illustrations in the margins. Decide if that is a feature you would use. Check to see if the print is large enough for you to read easily.

Decide on how you will use this dictionary. Do you want a paperback dictionary to put in your backpack? Or is this going to be the dictionary for your desk and a large hardback version would be the better choice? Several disciplines have specialized dictionaries with meanings that apply to those fields such as law or medicine. There are also bilingual dictionaries, such as French/English or Spanish/English, that can be helpful for school or travel. Take time in picking out your dictionary because a good dictionary will be a companion for years to come. A few dictionaries to consider are *Merriam-Webster's Collegiate Dictionary, The American Heritage Dictionary, The Random House College Dictionary,* and *The Oxford Dictionary.*

In general, when you are reading, try to use context clues, the words around the word you don't know, to first figure out the meaning of a word, but if you are still in doubt, don't hesitate to refer to a dictionary for the exact definition. Don't forget that dictionaries also contain more than definitions and are an essential reference source for any student.

Completing Analogies

An **analogy** shows a relationship between words. Working with analogies helps one to see connections between items, which is a crucial critical thinking skill. Analogies are written as follows: big : large :: fast : quick. The colon (:) means *is to*. The analogy reads big *is to* large as fast *is to* quick. To complete analogies there are two steps to follow:

1. find a relationship between the first pair of words
2. look for a similar relationship in another set of words

In the example above, *big* and *large* have similar meanings; they are synonyms. *Fast* and *quick* also have similar meanings, so the relationship between the four words uses synonyms.

Common relationships used in analogies (with examples) include

synonyms (trip : journey)   grammatical structure (shaking : shivering)

antonyms (real : fake)   cause and effect (step in a puddle : get wet)

examples (strawberry : fruit)   sequences (turn on car : drive)

part to a whole (handle : cup)   an object to a user or its use (spatula : chef)

Analogies in this book come in matching and fill-in-the-blank forms. Try the following analogies for practice.

Matching ||||||||||||||||||||||||||||||||||||||||||||||||||||||||||||||||||||||||||||||||||||||||

1. old : young :: _____   a. preface : book

2. clip coupons : go shopping :: _____   b. put on shoes : take a walk

3. peel : banana :: _____   c. low wages : strike

4. no rain : drought :: _____   d. rested : tired

Fill-in-the-Blank ||||||||||||||||||||||||||||||||||||||||||||||||||||||||||||||||||||||||||||||

writer	passion	abduct	sadly

5. frozen : chilled :: kidnap : _____

6. interrupting : rude :: embracing : _____

7. slow : slowly :: sad : _____

8. baton : conductor :: computer : _____

Answers

1. To figure out this analogy, first one needs to see that *old* and *young* are opposites, or **antonyms.** Next look at the choices and see if another pair of words are antonyms, and, yes, *rested* and *tired* are opposites. The answer is d.
2. A person would *clip coupons* and then *go shopping,* so there is a **sequence** of events. Of the choices, one would *put on shoes* and then *take a walk,* another sequence. The answer is b.
3. A *peel* is a part of a *banana,* while a *preface* is part of a *book,* so the connection is **part to a whole.** The answer is a.
4. When an area gets *no rain,* it can lead to a *drought,* and when people get paid *low wages,* they can go on *strike.* The connection among these pairs is **cause and effect.** The answer is c.
5. *Frozen* and *chilled* have similar meanings; they are **synonyms.** To solve the analogy, pick a word that has a similar meaning to *kidnap,* which would be *abduct.*
6. *Interrupting* a person is **an example** of a *rude* behavior. *Embracing* is an example of another type of behavior; in this case, it fits as an example of *passion.*
7. *Slow* is an adjective, and *slowly* an adverb; *sad* is an adjective, and *sadly* an adverb. This analogy works by using the same **grammatical structure** between the words.
8. A *baton* is used by a *conductor.* Who uses a *computer?* Among the choices, *writer* obviously fits. The relationship here is **object to user.**

   Sometimes you may come up with a relationship between the first two words that makes sense but doesn't fit any of the choices. Look at the choices and the two words again to see if you can find a way any four words fit together. Also do any obvious matches first, and with fewer choices it will be easier to spot the harder connections. Doing analogies can be fun as you begin to make clever connections and see word relationships in new ways. Finding word connections will help your brain make other connections in areas as diverse as writing essays, doing math problems, and arranging travel plans. Analogies are just another way to exercise your thinking skills.
   Try a few more analogies, and check your answers on page 12 to see how you did.

Matching

1. button : shirt ::   _____   a. broom : janitor

2. map : traveler ::   _____   b. drawer : desk

3. calm : tranquil ::   _____   c. stayed up late : exhausted

4. watched a comedy : laughed ::   _____   d. wise : smart

Fill-in-the-Blank

| huge | beverage | warmth | sleep |

5. make dinner : eat :: put on pajamas : _____
6. dull : bright :: tiny : _____
7. trunk : storage :: coat : _____
8. the Nile : a river :: iced tea : _____

Benefits of Flash Cards

There are several benefits to using flash cards to help you study vocabulary words.

Making the Cards   The first benefit comes from just making the cards. When you make a card, you will practice writing the word and its definition. You may also write a sentence using the word, record its part of speech, or draw a picture of the word. See the section "Create Your Own Flash Cards" on page 180 at the back of this book for ideas on how to make flash cards. Creating the cards allows for a personal experience with the words, which makes learning the words easier.

Working with Others   Another benefit is that using the cards can lead to collaborative activities. When you ask a friend, family member, or classmate to quiz you on the words, you get the chance to work with someone else, which many people enjoy. You may even establish a study group with the friends you find from quizzing each other on your flash cards.

Evaluating Your Learning   A third benefit is that the cards serve as pre-tests that let you evaluate how well you know a word. When a friend quizzes you, ask him or her to go over the words you miss several times. As the stack of flash cards with words you don't know gets smaller, you know that the words are becoming part of your vocabulary. You know that you are prepared to face a word on a quiz or test when you can correctly give the definition several times.

Making and using the flash cards should be fun. Enjoy the process of learning new words. Turn to the back of the book now to review the directions for creating flash cards, and you will be ready to make cards beginning with Chapter 1.

Word Wise Features

The Word Wise boxes share information on different areas related to vocabulary. There are seven types of features.

Internet Activity   suggests ways to use technology to enhance your learning experience.

A Different Approach   presents activities that you can do alone or collaboratively that allow you to interact with the vocabulary words using diverse methods, such as art, creative writing, and word groups. These other techniques can help to stimulate your mind and organize the vocabulary you are learning.

Context Clue Mini-Lessons   provide different types of context clue situations and give you the opportunity to practice using each type. *Context* means the words surrounding a specific word that give clues to that word's meaning. When you encounter a word whose meaning you don't know, keep reading the passage, looking for clues to help you figure out the meaning. These clues might be in the same sentence as the unknown words or in a sentence that comes before or after the word. Look for these types of clues in a passage:

Synonyms—words that have a similar meaning to the unknown word

Antonyms—words that mean the opposite of the unknown word

Examples—a list of items that explain the unknown word

General meaning—the meaning of the sentence or passage as a whole that could clarify the meaning of the unknown word

Each type of context clue has a mini-lesson, and a final lesson combines the methods. You will not find a context clue every time you encounter a word you don't know, but being aware of context clues will help you determine the meaning of many new words and make reading more enjoyable.

Interesting Etymologies presents notable word histories. Some of the histories use the word parts presented in the three Word Parts chapters of the text. Learning the history of a word can help you to remember its meaning.

Collocations show ways words are used together. The groupings can come in several forms, such as a verb with a noun (*commit* a *crime*), an adjective with a noun (*handsome stranger*), or a verb with a preposition (*come over*). Learning collocations will help you understand common ways to use the words you are studying. Sentences with the collocations in italics for some of the vocabulary words in this text are spread throughout the chapters. To become more familiar with collocations, look and listen for other repeated word combinations in the materials you read, in the phrases people use when speaking, and as you do the self-tests in this book.

Word Pairs illustrate how some words are often used near each other. Learning word pairs can help you to better remember both words. Some words are pairs because the items they represent are often used together, such as peanut butter and jelly. Other word pairs are opposites that are often found together when describing objects, actions, or people (such as "My friends are as different as night and day"). Word pairs are presented in several chapters with sample sentences to show how the words can be used near each other.

Connotations and Denotations examine reactions to a word. A **denotation** is "the explicit or direct meaning of a word." This is the kind of definition you would find in the dictionary. A **connotation** is "the suggestive or associative meaning of a word beyond its literal definition." This is the emotional response you have to a word. (A mnemonic device for remembering the difference between the two is that denotation begins with a "d," and it is the dictionary or direct meaning, both beginning with a "d").

It is important to realize that words have two kinds of meanings because careful writers use both kinds. You, as a writer and reader, want to make sure you are clearly expressing your point and understanding another writer's ideas by recognizing how words are used. Some connotations are personal reactions. For example, *seclusion* means "solitude; a sheltered place." Depending on your personality or current living conditions, you might picture *seclusion* as a wonderful chance to be alone and relax without all the chaos surrounding you, or if you hate being by yourself, you may envision it as a kind of torture separating you from friends and family. Other connotations have broader emotional responses. If you wanted to describe a thin person, you could use the words *slender* or *scrawny*. What do you picture in your mind for each word? Talk to your classmates about their images. Are they similar? Some words have positive connotations that people feel good about, and other words have negative connotations that turn people off. Not all words have strong connotations. For most people a pencil is a pencil, and there isn't much to get excited about. But other words can bring out strong feelings, such as *frugal*. The Connotation and Denotation lessons look at some of the vocabulary words in this text and the differences in their meanings.

Challenges Faced

Before the United States became a country, immigration was a part of the American experience. Tired of being **persecuted** for their religious beliefs, the
5 Pilgrims set sail from Plymouth, England, in 1620. They did not seek **martyrdom** by leaving England to settle in the New World, just the opportunity to freely practice their religion. The 101 passen-
10 gers faced being **destitute** as they left in September with two months of rough seas before them and arrival in a rugged, barely charted land as winter approached. Still, like future immigrants, they felt the

15 challenges were worth the rewards. They took animals and seed to start a new colony, and despite many hardships, they survived. A new country was set in motion, and settlers steadily continued arriving.

The nineteenth century was to see a period of mass migration. In 1846 the potato crop began to fail in Ireland, and economic and political problems hit other European countries. Many Europeans saw America as a place for **autonomy**. There they believed they would be free to start their own businesses or farms and
20 make their own religious and political decisions. Of course, many did not come without **ambivalence**. It was difficult to leave family, friends, and a way of life they had known for years. It was political oppression, starvation, and a hope for a better future for themselves and their children that **induced** most
25 people to come to America. Records show close to 24 million people arrived in the United States between 1880 and 1920. An immigration period of such **magnitude** has not been repeated in the United States.

Most immigrants have done their **utmost** to find a place in
30 American society. Balancing a respect for their original country with their new homes has not always been easy. Maybe one of the hardest aspects has been **placating** the second and third generations who have not always understood the traditions of their parents and grandparents as they try to fit into
35 American life. Many young people wonder why they must wear traditional clothing to celebrate holidays whose significance they don't really understand or why they must eat traditional foods when they want hamburgers and French fries. But these conflicts tend to resolve themselves with time as fami-
40 lies **ascertain** how to combine customs from the old country with new ones from America to form a multicultural society, taking the best from the many lands that make up this New World.

Predicting

For each set, write the definition on the line next to the word to which it belongs. If you are unsure, return to the reading on page 8, and underline any context clues you find. After you've made your predictions, check your answers against the Word List on page 13. Place a checkmark in the box next to each word whose definition you missed. These are the words you'll want to study closely.

Set One

poor	having conflicting feelings	harassed	extreme suffering	independence

❑ 1. **persecuted** (line 4) _____

❑ 2. **martyrdom** (line 6) _____

❑ 3. **destitute** (line 10) _____

❑ 4. **autonomy** (line 19) _____

❑ 5. **ambivalence** (line 21) _____

Set Two

maximum	persuaded	calming
to find out definitely	greatness in significance, size, or rank	

❑ 6. **induced** (line 24) _____

❑ 7. **magnitude** (line 27) _____

❑ 8. **utmost** (line 29) _____

❑ 9. **placating** (line 32) _____

❑ 10. **ascertain** (line 40) _____

Self-Tests

1 Finish these fictitious historical sentences. The year the sentence relates to is given in parentheses. Use each word once.

VOCABULARY LIST

autonomy	placated	magnitude	persecuted	ambivalence
destitute	utmost	ascertained	induced	martyrdom

1. The _____ of the American colonists is over. Yesterday's Boston Tea Party shows the British what we think of taxation without representation. (1773)

2. Explorers Lewis and Clark report that the _____ of the West is "amazing." (1806)

3. President Lincoln has been trying his _____ to keep the Union together. (1860)

4. Sitting Bull leads _____ Indians into battle at Little Bighorn. (1876)

| autonomy | placated | magnitude | persecuted | ambivalence |
| destitute | utmost | ascertained | induced | martyrdom |

5. Yesterday's earthquake in San Francisco has left thousands of citizens _____. (1906)

6. Another suicide has been _____ by the recent stock market crash. A man jumped to his death from a fifth-story window today. (1929)

7. Sources have _____ that Adolph Hitler's ultimate goal is world domination. The United States prepares to enter the war. (1941)

8. Those involved in isolated incidents of bra burnings say that the act symbolizes women's _____. (1968)

9. The American people will not be _____ by empty promises. Polls report that President Nixon must resign. (1974)

10. A recent study shows that the prevalence and sometimes misuse of cell phones and computers has lead to a(n) _____ in some Americans about the benefits of technology. (2006)

2 Match the historical event to the rest of the sentence that completes the idea about the event's significance. You may need to do some research or consult a dictionary.

_____ 1. Landing on the moon

_____ 2. The Great Depression

_____ 3. The Civil War

_____ 4. The Declaration of Independence

_____ 5. The Salem witch trials

_____ 6. The discovery of gold at Sutter's Fort

_____ 7. The invention of the automobile

_____ 8. The Nineteenth Amendment

_____ 9. Prohibition

_____ 10. Building the Panama Canal

a. has created feelings of ambivalence depending on whether one is stuck in gridlock or enjoying the open road.

b. was fought because the South wanted autonomy.

c. led to martyrdom for those who would not admit to powers they didn't have or acts they didn't do.

d. left millions of people destitute.

e. was of the utmost concern because it took a ship two months to sail from the Pacific Ocean to the Atlantic Ocean during the Spanish-American War.

f. was a document of such magnitude that it led to the formation of a new country.

g. tried to placate concerns about the evils of drinking.

h. helped scientists ascertain what it is made of.

i. gave women the right to vote, ending years of persecution.

j. induced money-hungry people to head to California.

3 Use the vocabulary words to complete the following analogies. For instructions, see Completing Analogies on page 4.

VOCABULARY LIST

| induce | persecute | destitute | martyrdom | ascertain |
| placate | utmost | magnitude | autonomy | ambivalence |

---

1. soft : hard :: anger : _____
2. dying for a belief : _____ :: hitting a pothole : car problems
3. confused : disturbed :: _____ : poor
4. _____ : least :: fresh : stale
5. an interview : nervousness :: going away to college : _____
6. _____ : the truth :: catch : a train
7. performer : audience :: teenager : some _____
8. hang : a painting :: _____ : labor
9. harass : _____ :: gentle : meek
10. feather : light :: The Great Barrier Reef : _____

Word Wise

Context Clue Mini-Lesson 1

This lesson features synonyms—words that have a similar meaning to the unknown word. In the paragraph below, circle the synonyms you find for the underlined words, and write them on the lines that follow the paragraph.

The din in the convention hall was deafening. Every vendor loudly touted the benefits of his or her product. The sellers pushed their products with phrases like the "best knife ever" or "lose ten pounds overnight." My friend admired the pluck of the sellers, but their shouts were nothing but noise to me. Many people also seemed to appreciate the spirited calls of the vendors as they gathered round to watch a demonstration. On the other hand, I began to rue the day I let my friend talk me into coming. My regret increased when, in a weak moment, I bought a hammer that was supposed to pound a nail with one blow.

The Synonym

1. Din _____

2. Touted _____

3. Pluck _____

4. Rue _____

Interactive Exercise

Answer the following questions dealing with U.S. history.

1. Name two groups that have been persecuted. _____

    _____

2. Name two situations that have induced people to fight for changes in laws.

    _____   _____

3. The magnitude of the car's influence on American life continues to this day. Give three examples of its effects. _____

    _____

4. What are two kinds of autonomy people have fought for?

    _____   _____

5. Name an event that you think must have caused ambivalence in some people.

    _____

6. Name two events that have made people destitute.

    _____   _____

7. What are two possible actions the government can take to placate angry citizens?

    _____   _____

8. Which invention do you think has had the utmost influence on society? Why?

    _____

    _____

9. Name two ways you could ascertain which candidate you should vote for in the next election for mayor or governor.

    _____

    _____

10. What two beliefs might a person hold that could lead to martyrdom?

    _____

    _____

HINT

Flash Cards

Flash cards are a great way to study vocabulary. Turn to the "Create Your Own Flash Cards" section at the end of this book (page 180) for suggestions on ways to make and use flash cards. Remember to carry your flash cards with you and study for at least a few minutes each day. Also ask classmates, friends, and family members to quiz you using the flash cards.

Answers to the analogies practice in the Getting Started section on page 5:

1. b   2. a   3. d   4. c   5. sleep   6. huge   7. warmth   8. beverage

Word List

ambivalence
[am biv′ ə ləns]
n. having conflicting feelings, such as love and hate, about a person, object, or idea

ascertain
[as′ ər tān′]
v. to find out definitely; to learn with certainty

autonomy
[ô ton′ ə mē]
n. independence; the quality of being self-governing

destitute
[des′ tə tōot′]
adj. devoid; poor; impoverished

induce
[in dōos′]
v. to persuade; to cause

magnitude
[mag′ ni tōod′]
n. greatness in significance, size, or rank

martyrdom
[mär′ tər dəm]
n. 1. extreme suffering
2. the state of being a martyr (one who chooses death or makes a sacrifice rather than give up religious faith or other belief)

persecute
[pûr′ sə kyōot′]
v. to harass; to annoy continuously

placate
[plā′ kāt′, plak′ āt′]
v. to pacify; to calm

utmost
[ut′ mōst′]
n. the greatest amount or level; maximum
adj. most extreme; of the greatest degree

Words to Watch

Which words would you like to practice with a bit more? Pick 3–5 words to study, and list them below. Write the word and its definition, and compose your own sentence using the word correctly. This extra practice could be the final touch to learning a word.

Word	Definition	Your Sentence
1. _____	_____	_____
2. _____	_____	_____
3. _____	_____	_____
4. _____	_____	_____
5. _____	_____	_____

2

Composition

The Midterm

Review Tips

Next week is the in-class essay midterm. To help you prepare for it, this sheet reviews some of the important concepts we have covered so far this semester. You will be writing about one of the four short stories we have read in the last two weeks. You will be explaining how the story is significant to today's world even though it was written more than one hundred years ago.

5

1. Make your **thesis** clear. The reader should know what your proposal is within the first or second paragraph of your essay. Your **intention** is to convince your reader that this short story is still important to read because it relates in one or more ways to society today.

10

2. You may need to **refute** other points of view. Think about ways an opponent might disagree with you and show how his or her view isn't as strong as yours.

3. Make your examples **vivid**. Pick scenes from the story that dramatically support your view. Pick examples from today's world that clearly show a connection to the events or ideas in the short story.

15

4. Remember the importance of **coherence** as you organize your essay. Pick a method of organization that allows the reader to clearly follow each of your points, and make sure each of your examples relates to your thesis.

5. Watch your **diction**. Your choice of words helps to set the tone of your essay. This is a formal essay, so you should avoid using slang words or other informal types of language.

20

6. You will need to **cite** passages from the story in your paper. As you **annotate** the story, look for lines and scenes that will help to make your point. Write comments in the margins, star important passages, and underline sections you may want to quote or **paraphrase**. You do not want to **plagiarize** any passages, so be sure to record the page number in parentheses after any quotations or paraphrases you use. Stealing other people's words or ideas is a serious offense that can get you expelled from college. Below are examples of quoting and paraphrasing to remind you of the correct formats.

25

Quotation: Use the writer's own words, and put the words in quotation marks.

The reader becomes skeptical of the narrator's sanity when he reveals his reason for committing murder: "Whenever it fell upon me, my blood ran cold; and so by degrees—very gradually—I made up my mind to take the life of the old man, and thus rid myself of the eye forever" (Poe 2).

30

Paraphrase: Put the writer's words into your own words, and do not use quotation marks.

The narrator says he isn't mad, but the reader begins to wonder how sane he can be when he reveals that he slowly decides to kill the old man because he is terrorized by the old man's eye (Poe 2).

35

If you take the time to prepare for the in-class essay by rereading the short stories, marking important passages in the stories, and thinking about how the stories relate to today's world, you should have no problem in writing your essay.

Predicting

For each set, write the definition on the line next to the word to which it belongs. If you are unsure, return to the reading on page 14, and underline any context clues you find. After you've made your predictions, check your answers against the Word List on page 19. Place a checkmark in the box next to each word whose definition you missed. These are the words you'll want to study closely.

Set One

| to disprove | | a plan | consistency | clear or dramatic |
| a proposal that is defended by argument | | | | |

- ☐ 1. **thesis** (line 8) _____
- ☐ 2. **intention** (line 9) _____
- ☐ 3. **refute** (line 11) _____
- ☐ 4. **vivid** (line 13) _____
- ☐ 5. **coherence** (line 15) _____

Set Two

| to quote as an example or expert | the choice and use of words | to make notes or comments on |
| to use the words or ideas of someone else as one's own | | to express in other words |

- ☐ 6. **diction** (line 18) _____
- ☐ 7. **cite** (line 20) _____
- ☐ 8. **annotate** (line 20) _____
- ☐ 9. **paraphrase** (line 22) _____
- ☐ 10. **plagiarize** (line 23) _____

Self-Tests

1 Circle the correct meaning of each vocabulary word.

1. cite:	to exaggerate	to quote
2. diction:	choice of words	choice of type size
3. plagiarize:	to quote	to steal
4. paraphrase:	to use an author's words	to express in other words
5. refute:	to disprove a statement	to agree with a statement
6. annotate:	to write a book	to make notes in a book
7. coherence:	illogical organization	orderly relationship
8. vivid:	brilliant	dull
9. intention:	a plan	clueless
10. thesis:	a proposal	a refusal

2 Match a word to each example. Use each word once.

VOCABULARY LIST

annotate	vivid	paraphrase	diction	plagiarize
cite	refute	thesis	intention	coherence

1. Shirley Jackson's story begins pleasantly: "The morning of June 27th was clear and sunny, with the fresh warmth of a full-summer day" (3). _____

2. a neon green skirt worn with a dazzling pink blouse _____

3. According to Austen, it isn't how long it takes but how good it is that matters. _____

4. I *really want* a new car. I *desire* a new car. I *need* a new car. _____

5. To put it in my own words, ask not what your country can do for you, but what you can do for your country. _____

6. *Good example of the boy's home life; Clear relationship here to incidents in par. 3*_____

7. Some people in the company believe the change in policy is causing problems, but they need to look ahead and see that, after some initial scheduling problems, all employees will have more time to spend on leisure pursuits. For example, when the rotation begins...._____

8. The school needs to offer more math classes so that students can graduate on time. _____

9. The plan is to get up at 6:00 and be on the road by 6:30. _____

10. Outline: Summer can cause special problems for some people. _____

    I. A greater chance of getting sunburned

   II. Dehydration

  III. Heat exhaustion

3 Finish the sentences using the vocabulary words. Use each word once.

VOCABULARY LIST

refuted	thesis	plagiarize	paraphrase	cite
vivid	diction	coherence	intention	annotate

1. My niece has a(n) _____ imagination. She can turn a tree and a stick into a castle and a wand and spend hours in her fairy kingdom.

2. The _____ of my research paper is that more Neighborhood Watch programs will make our city safer.

3. Because I was writing for children, I paid extra attention to my _____. I didn't want to use words they wouldn't understand.

4. I was confused when reading Isabel's paper because it lacked _____. First she told about a trip to a farm, and then she described her math test, and her topic was supposed to be about a favorite building.

5. It can be hard to _____ because you want to get the writer's idea correct, but you can't use any of the writer's key words or the same sentence pattern.

6. When I _____ a reading, I make comments on what I like and dislike, as well as marking important scenes and noting questions that I might want to bring up in a class discussion.

7. The _____ of the orientation meeting was to help students understand the campus, not to confuse them.

8. I thought my idea for the party was the best, but after Tony _____ my points, I saw how expensive and impractical my plan was.

9. I didn't mean to _____, but I didn't take very good notes, and I used the author's words four separate times without putting quotation marks around those passages.

10. My sister says she is never late; however, I can _____ four times she was late in the last two weeks.

Word Wise

Collocations

The *magnitude of the problem* unfolded as the day went on. One malfunction led to the creation of several other troubles. (Chapter 1)

This project is *of the utmost importance,* so I want you to devote all of your energy to it. (Chapter 1)

It is my *intention to* be the first in line at the Grand Opening Sale tomorrow. (Chapter 2)

You should be able to easily identify the *thesis statement* in each of the three essays we will be reading now that you know what to look for. (Chapter 2)

Connotations and Denotations

Martyrdom (Chapter 1): denotation—"the state of being a martyr (one who chooses death or makes a sacrifice rather than give up religious faith or other belief)." The connotation of martyrdom and martyr can take two forms. Many see martyrs as brave people who stand up for what they believe in. Others see a martyr as either a fool who won't make compromises to fit in or as a person who actually desires some kind of fame by choosing death. How do you view martyrdom? Is it a grand ideal or a crazy idea?

Interesting Etymologies

Plagiarize (Chapter 2): comes from the Latin *plagium,* "kidnapping," which comes from *plaga* meaning "net or snare." Obviously the meaning "to use the words or ideas of someone else as one's own" is an example of kidnapping. The word has been in use since the late 1500s.

Vivid (Chapter 2): comes from the Latin *vividus,* "spirited, lively," which comes from *vivus,* "alive." The word originated in the early 1600s. In reference to colors, its first use is recorded in 1665. The use of the word to mean "active or lively" when referring to the imagination or an interest in something is first reported in 1853.

Briefly annotate the following passage. Then write a paragraph where your thesis explains whether you would want to read the rest of this story based on this paragraph from page one. Circle your thesis. Cite a line from the passage, and paraphrase another line to help support your view. Don't forget to make your intention clear, use coherence throughout the paragraph, and use vivid examples to explain your position. Decide if you want the paragraph to sound formal or informal, as that will influence your diction.

The sky was gray, and thunder sounded in the distance. It was almost nightfall, and Helena was far from a place to rest. She had hoped to make it to her aunt's house before dark, but the adventure by the river had slowed her down. She hadn't expected to meet a family of trolls underneath the bridge. She had always thought the stories about trolls were ridiculous, but today she discovered that they could be true. The trolls had actually been quite nice. They even offered her homemade cookies. Though she hadn't really believed in trolls, if she did, she wouldn't have imagined them baking cookies. A streak of lightening lit up the sky, and the next blast of thunder sounded closer. Then the rain began to pour. Helena ran to a nearby tree, whose branches protected her from the rain. She took the last chocolate chip cookie out of her pocket and nibbled on it as she contemplated what to do next.

_____

_____

_____

_____

_____

_____

_____

_____

_____

_____

HINT

Study Often

Don't try to fit all of your studying into one session before a test. Look at your notes for a class often. Review them the day you write them while the information is fresh in your mind in case you want to add some material. Do a weekly review of material so that, as you learn new material, you can build on the old information. These same ideas apply to learning vocabulary. Look often at the flash cards you make. Even taking ten minutes a day to go over the words for that week will help you remember the meanings. While you are waiting for another class to start, for a friend who is late, or for the bus to come, take some of that time to review the words.

Word List

annotate
[an′ ō tāt′]
   v. to make notes or comments on or in the margins (usually in reference to a book)

cite
[sīt]
   v. 1. to quote as an example or expert
       2. to give as support or proof

coherence
[kō hēr′ əns, kō her′-]
   n. the quality of a logical or orderly relationship of parts; consistency; unity

diction
[dik′ shən]
   n. 1. the choice and use of words in speech or writing
       2. distinctness of speech

intention
[in ten′ shən]
   n. a plan; an aim that guides action

paraphrase
[par′ ə frāz′]
   v. to express in other words
   n. a restatement of a passage using other words

plagiarize
[plā′ jə rīz′]
   v. to use the words or ideas of someone else as one's own; to steal from another's writing

refute
[ri fyo͞ot′]
   v. to disprove; to show that a person or statement is wrong by argument or proof

thesis
[thē′ sis]
   n. a proposal that is defended by argument

vivid
[viv′ id]
   adj. 1. clear; striking; dramatic
       2. brilliant; having extremely bright colors
       3. active; lively

Words to Watch

Which words would you like to practice with a bit more? Pick 3–5 words to study, and list them below. Write the word and its definition, and compose your own sentence using the word correctly. This extra practice could be the final touch to learning a word.

	Word	Definition	Your Sentence
1.			
2.			
3.			
4.			
5.			

Mathematics

Work It Out

Complete the questions on this introductory worksheet by the next class meeting. These topics will be the focus of the class for the first half of the semester. Bring any concerns you have about these exercises to the next class meeting, or stop by during my office hours.

5

1. The company's monthly **quota** is 800 units. Use the following graph to answer the questions about the company.

    A. How many months has the company met its allowance? _____

    B. Use **statistics** to show how far the company was below its quota for March. _____

    C. Which month was the company 50% below its quota? _____

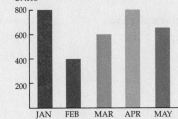

10

2. Use the following prices to figure out the **mean**, **median**, and mode for a pair of pants at a local department store.

    $12, $20, $20, $25, $30, $44, $59

    A. Mean, or average (add up all the numbers and divide by the number of items) _____

    B. Median (or middle number) _____

15

    C. Mode (the number that appears the most often) _____

3. **Calculate** what the **variable** x and the variable y stand for in the following equations.

    A. $3 + x + 6 = 14$ x = _____

    B. $4y + 11 = 27$ y = _____

    C. $2x - 6 = 60$ x = _____

20

4. Use the lines to the right to answer the following questions.

    A. Next to each line, indicate whether the line is **horizontal**, vertical, or diagonal.

    B. Use the variable A to indicate where two lines **intersect** and the variable B to show where three lines cross.

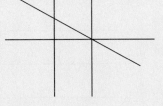

25

    C. Label the **parallel** lines C.

5. Which of the following shapes is **symmetrical**? _____

    Does the balanced shape cause a different reaction in you than the other shape? If it does, why do you think that might be so? _____

A.

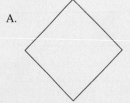

B.

Predicting |||||||||||||||||||||||||||||||||||||||||||||||||||||||||||||||||||||||||||||||||||||||||||||||||||

For each set, write the definition on the line next to the word to which it belongs. If you are unsure, return to the reading on page 20, and underline any context clues you find. After you've made your predictions, check your answers against the Word List on page 25. Place a checkmark in the box next to each word whose definition you missed. These are the words you'll want to study closely.

Set One

> numerical facts   the middle number in a specified sequence of numbers   the average   to figure
>
> a part of a total amount or an allowance

❑   1.   **quota** (line 4) _____

❑   2.   **statistics** (line 7) _____

❑   3.   **mean** (line 10) _____

❑   4.   **median** (line 10) _____

❑   5.   **calculate** (line 16) _____

Set Two

> balanced   lines that go in the same direction and never meet   to cross   parallel to level ground
>
> a symbol that represents a changeable amount

❑   6.   **variable** (line 16) _____

❑   7.   **horizontal** (line 21) _____

❑   8.   **intersect** (line 23) _____

❑   9.   **parallel** (line 25) _____

❑   10.   **symmetrical** (line 26) _____

Self-Tests |||||||||||||||||||||||||||||||||||||||||||||||||||||||||||||||||||||||||||||||||||||||||||||||

1 Put a T for true or F for false next to each sentence.

_____   1. If a person decides to take a statistics class, it would help to be good at math.

_____   2. It is a good idea to calculate how much your purchases will be before you check out to make sure you have enough money.

_____   3. The mean for the three ages 11, 19, and 33 is 21.

_____   4. Having a small triangle on one side of a picture and five large circles on the other side would be a symmetrical arrangement.

_____   5. The weather in the United States is rarely variable.

_____   6. Elevators usually travel horizontally.

_____   7. The parallels between pyramid designs in Egypt and Central America have caused some people to speculate that the pyramids were built by aliens.

_____   8. When a vertical and a horizontal line cross, they intersect.

_____ 9. It could be difficult to fill one's quota of strawberries to be picked if the person stops to eat several every five minutes.

_____ 10. The median number in the following series is 9: 2, 4, 9, 12, 15, 23, 35.

2 Complete each sentence using the vocabulary words. Use each word once.

VOCABULARY LIST

calculate	horizontal	intersect	quota	symmetrical
mean	median	parallel	statistics	variable

1. The most recent _____ show that enrollment is up 20% in all math classes this semester compared with the last two semesters.

2. Our study showed that people were more attracted to the display with the _____ design than to the one with the irregular pattern.

3. From my past experiences of driving north, I _____ that it will take us nine hours to reach Grandma's house.

4. When I worked in retail, my hours were _____. I started anywhere between 7 a.m. and 6 p.m., and I worked from four to eight hours a day.

5. The new road has been designed to _____ the town, so tourists have to come right through downtown, and we hope that will cause them to stop and do some shopping or spend the night.

6. As soon as I got my _____ of donations for the auction, I quit asking. Even though it is for a worthy cause, I am not really comfortable asking businesses to contribute items.

7. The _____ house price in our city has dropped 30% in the last year.

8. I was offered a(n) _____ transfer at work. I would have stayed at the same level but would have been in a different department. Because I like the people I work with now, I turned it down.

9. The _____ structures, so perfectly spaced in the park, make for an ideal passageway.

10. I calculated the _____ for my math test scores by dividing the sum of my scores by the number four (that is how many tests we have had), and I am averaging 87%.

3 Complete the following analogies. See Completing Analogies on page 4 for instructions and practice.

VOCABULARY LIST

parallel	horizontal	intersect	median	symmetrical
mean	quota	calculate	statistics	variable

1. long : short :: vertical : _____
2. skyscrapers : tall :: interest rates : _____
3. old : elderly :: compute: _____
4. boring : exciting :: unbalanced : _____
5. 10, 15, 20, 24, 43, 56 = 22 : _____ :: poodle : dog
6. portion : _____ :: silence : hush
7. hem : a skirt :: _____ : a circle
8. railroad tracks : _____ :: fog : weather
9. house : home :: average : _____
10. government : _____ :: cook : stove

Word Wise

Collocations

The pilot took a *calculated risk* and landed the plane in an onion field minutes before running out of fuel. (Chapter 3)

The *median income* for a job as a teacher in my state is $35,000 a year. (Chapter 3)

I am enjoying the story line about the *parallel universe* more than the one about life on Earth in the recent Tremendous Team comic book series. (Chapter 3)

Word Pairs

Symmetrical/Asymmetrical: Symmetrical (Chapter 3) means "balanced." Asymmetrical means "unbalanced; irregular." The symmetrical building attracted people to its graceful design. The asymmetrical building shocked people and displeased several of them.

Connotations and Denotations

Quota (Chapter 3): denotation—"the number or percentage of people of a specified type allowed into a group." In recent years, quota systems have upset people, and *quota* has taken on a negative connotation for many people. How do you feel when you hear that a college or other organization must fulfill a quota for admitting people?

Interactive Exercise |||||||||||||||||||||||||||||||||||||||||||||||||||||||||||||||||||||||||||||||||||||||||||||||||

Answer the following questions to practice using the vocabulary words.

Imagine you eat lunch out Monday through Friday for a week. On Monday, you have a tuna sandwich that costs $6.60; on Tuesday, teriyaki chicken for $6.00; on Wednesday, curry for $5.20; on Thursday, a burrito for $4.80; and on Friday, a slice of pizza for $2.40. Use this information to answer the following questions.

1. Calculate the median price of your five meals. _____

2. Calculate the mean price of your five meals. _____

3. Supply the answers for these statistics:
   A. One day you spend 50% less than on the previous day. Which day was that? _____
   B. One day you spent 10% more than on the following day. Which day was that? _____

4. If your quota for meals out a month is 18, and, so far this month, you have eaten out four other times besides the five times this week, what percentage of your quota have you used up? _____

5. Calculate what the variable x stands for in these equations:

   A. Monday's meal + Friday's meal + x = $15.00
      x = _____ (which day's meal)
   B. A burrito + curry − x = $7.60
      x = _____ (which food item)

Answer the following questions about the sketch of the house.

6. How many horizontal lines are in the frame of the house? _____

7. How many sets of parallel lines are in the frame of the house? _____

8. What are two symmetrical elements of the house? _____ _____

9. What area of the front yard does the entrance pathway intersect? _____

HINT

Multiple Meanings

Most words have more than one meaning. For some words, one meaning is used more often than the others, but, for other words, two or three of their meanings are equally well used. For example, a bat is "a wooden club used to hit a ball" or "a mammal that flies, usually at night." Both meanings for bat are frequently used. However, among the meanings for *cure* as a noun, most people would know "a means of healing" and possibly "a process of preserving meat, fish, etc. by smoking, salting, or the like," but the meaning of "the office or district of a curate or parish priest" is not seen as often. This book usually gives alternate meanings as long as they are fairly common. One meaning will be used in the reading for the chapter, but the Self-Tests that follow the reading may use the additional meanings, so carefully look over the Word List before you start the Self-Tests. If you ever see a word used in a way you are not familiar with, check a dictionary to see if it has another meaning you do not know. You may be surprised at how many meanings even a short and seemingly simple word may have. *Webster's Collegiate Dictionary* lists twenty-four meanings for the word *so*. Just be prepared for the fun and challenges that multiple meanings provide.

Word List

calculate
[kal′ kyə lāt′]

v. to figure; to compute; to evaluate

horizontal
[hôr′ i zon′ tl, hor′-]

adj. 1. parallel to level ground
2. flat; at the same level

intersect
[in′ tər sekt′]

v. to cross; to meet at a point; to cut through

mean
[mēn]

n. the result found by dividing the sum of a set of numbers by the number of items in the set; the average
adj. holding a middle position

median
[mē′ dē ən]

n. the middle number in a specified sequence of numbers (if the sequence has an even number of numbers, the average of the two middle numbers)
adj. relating to or located in the middle

parallel
[par′ ə lel′]

adj. 1. lines that go in the same direction and never meet
2. alike in some form
n. a likeness

quota
[kwō′ tə]

n. 1. a part of a total amount; an allotment; an allowance
2. the number or percentage of people of a specified type allowed into a group

statistics
[stə tis′ tiks]

n. 1. (used with a plural v.) data; numerical facts
2. (used with a singular v.) the science that deals with the study of numerical data

symmetrical
[si me′ tri kəl]

adj. regular in arrangement of matching parts; balanced

variable
[vâr′ ē ə bəl]

n. 1. a symbol that represents a changeable amount
2. something that may change
adj. changeable; inconstant

Words to Watch

Which words would you like to practice with a bit more? Pick 3–5 words to study, and list them below. Write the word and its definition, and compose your own sentence using the word correctly. This extra practice could be the final touch to learning a word.

	Word	Definition	Your Sentence
1.	_____	_____	_____
	_____	_____	_____
2.	_____	_____	_____
	_____	_____	_____
3.	_____	_____	_____
	_____	_____	_____
4.	_____	_____	_____
	_____	_____	_____
5.	_____	_____	_____

A Walk in the Woods

Welcome to the Small Woods Nature Trail!

By using this guide, you will learn about the **flora** and **fauna** of the area. A variety of plants and animals live in the woods and interact with each other in order to survive. Look for the numbered signposts that correspond with this guide. Enjoy your **sojourn** through the **myriad** wonders of nature!

Stop 1   In front of you is an example of a **parasitic** relationship. The mistletoe plant has attached itself to the oak tree and is using the moisture and food from the tree to feed itself. Sometimes the mistletoe can get so large that it ends up killing its host.

If you are here in the autumn, you will also see that the oak is losing its leaves. Most oak trees are **deciduous**, meaning they lose their leaves in the fall. You may not remember it, but you even had a deciduous part in your body. Baby teeth are also called deciduous teeth because they fall out as a part of the growing process.

Stop 2   In contrast to the parasitic relationship of the mistletoe and the oak tree, here you see a **symbiotic** relationship in the **lichen** growing on the rocks at your feet. Lichen are plants made up of a fungus and an alga growing together. The fungi use the food made by the algae, and the algae use the water absorbed by the fungi. The two materials help each other survive. Lichen grow on rocks and trees, and about sixteen thousand **species** have been identified. Some types of lichen are used as food by animals such as reindeer in the arctic areas and even by humans. Lichens are also used in making perfumes. As you continue your walk, look for the various colors of lichen from gray to green to white. When they are moist, the lichen are usually a bright green.

Stop 3   The pine trees around you are examples of evergreens. Unlike deciduous trees, the leaves of evergreens stay green all year.

Stop 4   At the right time of year, you can enjoy the beauty of butterflies fluttering around you. Butterflies go through a four-stage **metamorphosis**. They go from egg to larva (a caterpillar) to pupa (the resting stage) to adult. The colorful butterflies you see are in the adult stage. Butterflies are useful to the woods as they often pollinate flowers.

5

10

15

20

25

30

Predicting

For each set, write the definition on the line next to the word to which it belongs. If you are unsure, return to the reading on page 26, and underline any context clues you find. After you've made your predictions, check your answers against the Word List on page 31. Place a checkmark in the box next to each word whose definition you missed. These are the words you'll want to study closely.

Set One

| a temporary stay | living off another species | animals | plants | innumerable |

☐ 1. **flora** (line 2) _____

☐ 2. **fauna** (line 2) _____

☐ 3. **sojourn** (line 4) _____

☐ 4. **myriad** (line 4) _____

☐ 5. **parasitic** (line 5) _____

Set Two

| a change in form | shedding the leaves annually | organisms having some common qualities |
| pertaining to the living together of dissimilar organisms | | an organism composed of a fungus and an alga |

☐ 6. **deciduous** (line 10) _____

☐ 7. **symbiotic** (line 16) _____

☐ 8. **lichen** (line 16) _____

☐ 9. **species** (line 21) _____

☐ 10. **metamorphosis** (line 31) _____

Self-Tests

1 Circle the word that best completes each sentence.

1. My (sojourn, myriad) in the Amazon only lasted five weeks, but I loved every minute of it.

2. After just three days of kindergarten, the child's (species, metamorphosis) from being extremely afraid to feeling confident was amazing.

3. The (fauna, flora) in the desert, from the brittle bush to the ocotillo plant, really bloom in the spring after a shower.

4. There were (parasitic, myriad) reasons why I was unable to make the meeting. I can't even start to tell you the problems I ran into that day.

5. The roommates' relationship became quite (symbiotic, parasitic) as they helped each other with homework and chores based on their strengths.

6. The (fauna, flora) in the woods include small animals such as squirrels and bigger animals like bears.

7. The (lichen, sojourn) covered the rocks and trees throughout the forest.

8. I think the autumn is a lovely time of year because the (parasitic, deciduous) trees in our neighborhood turn beautiful colors.

9. My friendship with Joanne started out well, but it has become (symbiotic, parasitic); all she does now is ask me for money and favors.

10. There are several (species, flora) of birds in the marsh, so we should have a great time bird watching this morning.

2 Finish the journal entries using the vocabulary words. Use each word once.

Set One

VOCABULARY LIST

lichen	species	myriad	deciduous	flora

October 10, 2008

My early morning hike in the forest was wonderful. The air was crisp, and wispy clouds blew across the sky. The (1)_____ trees are beginning to lose their leaves. Red, gold, and orange leaves carpeted the ground. The (2)_____ were a bright green in the morning mist. The (3)_____ had a magical quality: the flowers danced, and the trees whispered to me. Every (4)_____ of plant seemed to have some advice, from the oak telling me to be strong to the dandelion urging me to go where the wind takes me. (5)_____ possibilities opened before me as I strolled through nature's majesty.

Set Two

VOCABULARY LIST

metamorphosis	fauna	sojourn	parasitic	symbiotic

April 2, 2009

Today the first buds of spring are appearing on many of the trees. I am so lucky to be able to see the (6)_____ of the forest. I also spied a deer during my (7)_____. Of all the (8)_____ in the forest, the deer are my favorite. They are such beautiful creatures. I have always been afraid that my relationship with nature has been a (9)_____ one. I get so much enjoyment from plants and animals, but I have never felt that I have been able to give anything in return. Yesterday circumstances changed. I signed up to be a docent, and now the relationship can be (10)_____. I can still find peace from the forest, but I can also help to protect it by educating people about the joys of nature.

3 Match each item to the vocabulary word it best relates to. Use each word once.

VOCABULARY LIST

fauna	deciduous	lichen	flora	myriad
symbiotic	species	sojourn	parasitic	metamorphosis

1. pebbles on a beach, stars in the sky _____

2. ivy, roses _____

3. the homely girl in most teenage movies, moths _____

4. at the beach, to the mountains _____

5. maple trees, a stag's antlers _____

6. fox, squirrel _____

7. on rocks, on the sides of trees _____

8. the wood lily, the meadow lily _____

9. an unemployed relative who comes to stay and ends up watching television all day, fleas and ticks _____

10. the hermit crab and sea anemone, the white cattle egret and the elephant _____

Word Wise

Word Pairs

Flora/Fauna: Flora (Chapter 4) means "the plants of a given region or period taken as a whole." Fauna (Chapter 4) means "the animals of a given region or period taken as a whole." The flora in my neighborhood park mainly consists of cedars and ferns, and the most abundant fauna are squirrels and deer.

Parasitic/Symbiotic: Parasitic (Chapter 4) means "pertaining to a parasite, such as a person who takes advantage of others." On the other hand, symbiotic (Chapter 4) can mean "any mutually beneficial relationship." My last romance involved a parasitic relationship—all my girlfriend cared about was my money. I am now looking for a symbiotic relationship where we can share interests and emotions.

Interesting Etymologies

Parasite (Chapter 4): comes from the Greek *para,* "beside" and *sitos,* "grain or food." Together *parasitos* originally meant "fellow guest." It came to mean in ancient Greece a professional dinner guest who was invited to amuse or flatter the host. By the 1500s, the meaning had expanded to "a person who takes advantage of others," which today could still be by eating often at someone's house and not returning the favor.

Interactive Exercise |||||||||||||||||||||||||||||||||||||||||||||||||||||||||||||||||||||

Your biology class has just taken the walk through Small Woods. Your instructor has given you the following worksheet to complete.

Name _____

1. List two types of fauna and two types of flora that you saw.

   _____ _____ , _____ _____

2. Did you see any deciduous trees? How could you tell?

   _____

3. Where did you spot lichen? _____

4. Name two species you saw. _____ , _____

5. What is one metamorphosis that you would expect to see if we returned to the woods in the winter? _____

6. Describe how humans have had a parasitic relationship with nature. What can we do to make our relationship more symbiotic? _____

   _____

7. Of the myriad wonders of nature we saw, which most impressed you? _____

   _____

8. Where do you suggest our next sojourn take us? _____

Conversation Starters

An excellent way to review the vocabulary words and help to make them your own is to use them when you are speaking. Gather three to five friends or classmates, and use one or more of the conversation starters below. Before you begin talking, have each person write down six of the vocabulary words he or she will use during the conversation. Share your lists with each other to check that you did not all pick the same six words. Try to cover all of the words you want to study, whether you are reviewing one, two, or more chapters.

1. What do you consider two of the most significant events in American history? Why are these events so important?
2. Discuss what you like and don't like about the writing process.
3. How do you use math skills in your everyday life? Think about a variety of activities, from paying bills to going shopping.
4. Do you enjoy being out in nature? If you were going to take a sojourn, which environment would you prefer to visit: the mountains, the desert, or the beach? Why?

Word List

deciduous
[di sij′ o͞o əs]

adj. 1. shedding the leaves annually, as certain trees do
2. falling off at a particular stage of growth; transitory

fauna
[fô′ nə]

n. the animals of a given region or period taken as a whole

flora
[flôr′ ə, flōr′ ə]

n. the plants of a given region or period taken as a whole

lichen
[lī′ kən]

n. a complex organism composed of a fungus in symbiotic union with an alga, commonly forming patches on rocks and trees

metamorphosis
[met′ ə môr′ fə sis]

n. 1. a change in form from one stage to the next in the life of an organism
2. a transformation

myriad
[mir′ ē ad]

adj. of an indefinitely great number; innumerable
n. an immense number

parasitic
[par′ ə sit′ ik]

adj. pertaining to a parasite (1. an organism that lives on another species without aiding the host; 2. a person who takes advantage of others)

sojourn
[n. sō′ jûrn]
[v. sō jûrn′]

n. a temporary stay
v. to stay temporarily

species
[spē′ shēz, -sēz]

n. organisms having some common qualities; kind or type

symbiotic
[sim bē ot′ ik]

adj. 1. pertaining to the living together of two dissimilar organisms
2. any mutually dependent or beneficial relationship

Words to Watch

Which words would you like to practice with a bit more? Pick 3–5 words to study, and list them below. Write the word and its definition, and compose your own sentence using the word correctly. This extra practice could be the final touch to learning a word.

Word	Definition	Your Sentence
1.		
2.		
3.		
4.		
5.		

5

Word Parts I

Look for words with these **prefixes**, **roots**, and/or **suffixes** as you work through this book. You may have already seen some of them, and you will see others in later chapters. Learning basic word parts can help you figure out the meanings of unfamiliar words.

prefix: a word part added to the beginning of a word that changes the meaning of the root

root: a word's basic part with its essential meaning

suffix: a word part added to the end of a word; indicates the part of speech

Word Part	Meaning	Examples and Definitions
Prefixes		
ambi-	both, around	*ambivalence:* having conflicting feelings; feeling both ways *ambiance:* the atmosphere around a person
mag-	great, large	*magnitude:* greatness *magnify:* to make larger
post-	after, behind	*posterity:* future generations; those that come after *postdoctoral:* pertaining to study done after receiving a doctorate
Roots		
-duc-	to lead	*conducive:* leading toward *induce:* lead one to do
-lev-	lift, light, rise	*alleviate:* to lighten; to reduce *elevator:* a device that lifts people
-pon-, -pos-	to put, to place	*proponent:* one who puts one's point forward *juxtaposition:* an act of placing close together
-rog-	to ask	*prerogative:* a special right to ask for something *interrogate:* to ask questions
-vi-, -viv-	life, to live	*vivid:* filled with life; dramatic *revive:* to bring back to life
Suffixes		
-dom (makes a noun)	state, condition, or quality of	*martyrdom:* the state of suffering *freedom:* the condition of being free
-tude (makes a noun)	state or quality of	*magnitude:* the quality of being great *gratitude:* the state of being thankful

Self-Tests

1 Read each definition, and choose the appropriate word. Use each word once. The meaning of the word part is underlined to help you make the connection. Refer to the Word Parts list if you need help.

VOCABULARY LIST

survive	attitude	ambidextrous	levitate	postbellum
wisdom	conductor	deposit	prerogative	magnum

1. capable of using <u>both</u> hands _____
2. occurring <u>after</u> a war _____
3. the person who <u>leads</u> the orchestra _____
4. to <u>put</u> money in the bank _____
5. a special right to <u>ask</u> for something _____
6. to continue to <u>live</u> _____
7. a <u>large</u> wine bottle _____
8. a <u>state</u> of mind about something _____
9. the <u>quality of</u> having good judgment _____
10. to float or <u>lift</u> a person or thing _____

2 Finish the sentences with the meaning of each word part. Use each meaning once. The word part is underlined to help you make the connection.

VOCABULARY LIST

after	great	lead	life	rise
condition	put	ask	state of	around

1. She received a <u>post</u>humous award: it was given to her the year _____ she died.
2. My free<u>dom</u> is important to me. It is a(n) _____ that I don't take for granted.
3. I moved the <u>lev</u>er to make the door _____.
4. The police interro<u>g</u>ated the man for two hours; they had a lot of questions to _____.
5. My friends tried to se<u>duc</u>e me into going to the movies, but they couldn't _____ me astray; I stayed home and studied.
6. His answers were amb<u>i</u>guous: he kept dancing _____ my questions.
7. I transpo<u>s</u>ed the numbers on my check: I _____ the "1" before the "2" and ended up being <u>nine</u> dollars short.
8. Their house is <u>magni</u>ficent; everything about it is _____.
9. Katy is a con<u>viv</u>ial person; she is so sociable and full of _____.
10. In ancient Rome, captives often lived a life of servi<u>tude</u>; they spent the rest of their lives in a(n) _____ slavery.

3 Finish the story using the word parts below. Use each word part once. Your knowledge of word parts, as well as the context clues, will help you create the correct words. If you do not understand the meaning of a word you have made, check the dictionary for the definition or to see whether the word exists.

WORD PARTS

lev	ambi	viv	mag	duc
tude	post	pos	rog	dom

A Revealing Walk

After three days of snow and a six-hour power outage, the (1)_____ance in the apartment was rather unpleasant. We had been cooped up for too long. One roommate was beginning to make de(2)_____atory remarks about my hair, while I was insulting his taste in clothing. Our other roommate was curled up in the corner with a book in front of his face trying to ignore us. We were all suffering from bore(3)_____ and needed something to amuse ourselves.

    I decided it was best to ex(4)_____e myself to the elements as the snow was beginning to melt. When I first ventured out, I wondered what could have in(5)_____ed me to come out in the cold, but then I remembered our bickering, and I thought the walk was still a good idea. The air was fresh, and it felt good to be moving. As I looked at the splendor of the snow-covered trees, the (6)_____nitude of the problems in the apartment began to seem so small. Then I saw the flowers poking out of the snow. Their beauty re(7)_____ed my spirits. To see life blooming again made me happy. Maybe the long winter we had been having would soon be over. I felt such grati(8)_____ to the lovely flowers. The return of life made me think about (9)_____erity and what I most wanted to leave for future generations. Maybe the re(10)_____ance of a few flowers in the snow to the big issues of life and death wouldn't hit most people, but for some reason those flowers made me look at the world in a whole new way.

4 Pick the best definition for each underlined word using your knowledge of word parts. Circle the word part in each of the underlined words.

a. the state of having enough

b. a person who puts one's point forward

c. liveliness

d. the condition of being famous

e. surrounding

f. showing a great spirit

g. a raised area of earth along a river

h. to lead or bring in

i. assuming superior rights

j. examination of a body after death

_____ 1. Diana's vivacity kept the party alive: she danced and laughed all night.

_____ 2. The levee wasn't high enough to keep the water from flooding the houses.

_____ 3. The postmortem revealed that the man had been poisoned.

_____ 4. The arrogant man wanted everything done his way.

_____ 5. The magnanimous donation helped us build the hospital sooner than we expected.

_____ 6. Keri didn't let stardom go to her head. Even after appearing in three blockbuster movies, she was still the same sweet girl when she came home for the holidays.

_____ 7. The ambient music in the restaurant was supposed to be relaxing, but I found it annoying.

_____ 8. Four years after his retirement, the community decided it was time to induct Phillips into the local Sports Hall of Fame.

_____ 9. We have a plentitude of food for dinner with the pizza I got and the chicken you brought.

_____ 10. She was a proponent of the new park from the beginning; she continually let people know that the neighborhood kids needed a safe place to play.

5 A good way to remember word parts is to pick one word that uses a word part and understand how that word part functions in the word. Then you can apply that meaning to other words that have the same word part. Use the words to help you match the word part to its meaning.

Set One

_____ 1. **ambi-:** ambiguous, ambivalent, ambiance

_____ 2. **mag-:** magnificent, magnify, magnitude

_____ 3. **-dom:** martydom, freedom, wisdom

_____ 4. **-duc-:** induce, conductor, seduce

_____ 5. **-vi-, -viv-:** viable, vivid, revive

a. life, to live

b. to lead

c. state, condition, or quality of

d. both, around

e. great, large

Set Two

_____ 6. **-pon-, -pos-:** proponent, juxtaposition, deposit

_____ 7. **-lev-:** levity, levitate, elevator

_____ 8. **post-:** posterity, postdoctoral, posthumously

_____ 9. **-rog-:** interrogate, derogatory, prerogative

_____ 10. **-tude:** magnitude, gratitude, multitude

f. lift, light, rise

g. state or quality of

h. after, behind

i. to put, to place

j. to ask

Interactive Exercise |||||||||||||||||||||||||||||||||||||||||||||||||||||||||||||||||||||||||||||||||||||||

Use the dictionary to find a word you don't know that uses the word part listed below. Write the meaning of the word part, the word, and the definition. If your dictionary has the etymology (history) of the word, see how the word part relates to the meaning, and write the etymology after the definition.

Word Part	Meaning	Word	Definition and Etymology
EXAMPLE:			
mag-	great, large	magnifico	1. a Venetian nobleman
			2. any person of high rank
			(from Latin magnificus, magn(us)
			large, great)
1. ambi-			
2. -duc-			
3. -lev-			
4. post-			
5. -vi- or -viv-			

Word Wise

This lesson uses antonyms—words that mean the opposite of the unknown word—as the clues. Circle the antonyms you find for the underlined words and then write a word that is the opposite of the antonym as your definition of the word.

When I went to visit, Marsha's greeting was <u>cordial</u>. A few people had told me that she was often cold and unfriendly, but I did not find her so. We merrily chatted for an hour, when suddenly she cast an <u>aspersion</u> on my blouse. I thought she was going to compliment it when she mentioned the unusual color, but I was wrong. I was <u>dejected</u>. I had been so excited about making a new friend. What I had hoped to be the beginning of a new friendship turned out to be its <u>demise</u>.

Your Definition

1. Cordial _____

2. Aspersion _____

3. Dejected _____

4. Demise _____

HINT

Etymologies

An etymology is the history of a word. Some dictionaries will explain in an entry how the word came into existence. Words can be developed in several ways such as being made up, coming from a person's name, or evolving from foreign languages. Reading a word's etymology can sometimes help you remember the meaning. For example, the word **dismal** comes from the Latin *dies mali*. *Dies* is the plural of day and *mali* the plural of evil. In Middle English the word meant "unlucky days." There were two days in each month that were thought to be unfavorable, and it was believed a person shouldn't start anything important on those days. These days were even marked on calendars during the Middle Ages. For example, in March, the two days were the 1st and 28th, and in June, the days were the 10th and 16th. The word now means "causing depression or dread." It is easy to see how this definition came from the idea of unlucky days.

Not all words have interesting histories, but taking the time to read an etymology can be useful. If you get excited about word origins, there are books available on the subject that show how fascinating language can be.

Focus on Chapters 1–5

The following activities give you a chance to interact some more with the vocabulary words you've been learning. By looking at art, taking tests, answering questions, doing a crossword puzzle, and working with others, you will see which words you know well and which you still need to work with.

Art

Match each picture below to one of the following vocabulary words. Use each word once.

VOCABULARY LIST

annotate	lichen	parallel
placate	symmetrical	destitute

1. _____

2. _____

3. _____

4. _____

5. _____

6. _____

1 Pick the word that best completes each sentence.

1. My sister said she needed her _____, so she moved out of our apartment.

   a. diction   b. fauna   c. autonomy   d. median

2. I love the fall. The _____ trees are so beautiful as they drop their red, yellow, and brown leaves.

   a. horizontal   b. deciduous   c. utmost   d. parallel

3. I had a hard time deciding whether the frame looked better in a _____ or vertical position. Once I decided that I liked the red stripe at the top of the frame instead of on the side, I found a picture to put in it.

   a. horizontal   b. vivid   c. destitute   d. parasitic

4. I was shocked to learn that a bestselling author had _____ most of his last book from his brother's journals.

   a. persecuted   b. placated   c. intersected   d. plagiarized

5. There was a lack of _____ in my uncle's stories. He would begin by telling me about something that happened last week, and suddenly the story would shift to his childhood.

   a. statistics   b. magnitude   c. coherence   d. flora

2 Complete the following sentences using the vocabulary words. Use each word once.

a. martyrdom	b. thesis	c. species	d. flora	e. quota

1. So many _____ from panda bears to tigers are endangered these days due to loss of their natural habitats.

2. I had to revise my _____ after I discovered some new information on the topic.

3. I worked efficiently and met my _____ of phone calls to make about the upcoming election by noon.

4. The _____ in the mountains offer a gorgeous array of colors in the spring.

5. The days of _____ are not over. People are stilling willing to die for political and religious beliefs worldwide.

3 Finish the story using the vocabulary words. Use each word once.

Making a Quilt

When I was little, I would try to (1)_____ what my grandmother was doing in the back room of her house at night. She, however, would quickly see me open the door and shoo me back to bed. When I was about eight, the situation changed. My grandmother introduced me to her quilt making. She told me that her (2)_____ when I was small was not to be mean but to protect me and the quilts. She was afraid I might hurt myself with the needles or disrupt her system of laying out materials. Now she was happy to introduce me to the (3)_____ scraps she had collected over the years.

    I watched with some (4)_____ the first time she cut up one of my favorite childhood shirts. Part of me hated to see it destroyed, but I knew she was going to make it into something special. One of the first tasks I learned was to (5)_____ how many pieces I would need to make a quilt of a certain size. Then she taught me the various steps to perform the (6)_____ from scraps to blanket. I loved seeing the (7)_____ colors of the various pieces of clothing transform into something that for years would keep me warm on cold winter nights. To me, it was magical how she made the various shapes (8)_____. She could make so many (9)_____ patterns that I thought I would never be able to learn half of them. I tried my (10)_____ to become as good as she was. My needle skills never did match hers, but they aren't bad.

    Over the years, our relationship became quite (11)_____. As her eyesight failed, I helped her thread needles, and she taught me a wonderful skill while sharing priceless family history as we worked together. I would definitely (12)_____ those who say that children and grandparents can't find much in common these days. I had hours of enjoyment with my grandmother making our quilts, and I now share that joy with my granddaughter and grandson.

Interactive Exercise |||||||||||||||||||||||||||||||||||||||||||||||||||||||||||||||||||

Answer the following questions to further test your understanding of the vocabulary words.

1. What could induce you to do something you might not usually think of doing, like skydiving or going to the opera?

    _____

2. What are two examples of parasitic relationships?

    _____

    _____

3. Name a field that uses a lot of statistics.

    _____

4. Name two groups that are persecuted in today's world.

    _____

5. Cite two examples of successes you have had in college.

    _____

    _____

6. Name two types of fauna found in your city or town.

    _____

7. Write a list of five ages of people you know, and then calculate the median age.

    _____

8. Where would you like to sojourn during the summer? Why did you pick this place?

    _____

    _____

9. Paraphrase the following sentence: "At the right time of year, you can enjoy the beauty of butter-flies fluttering around you."

    _____

    _____

10. Give examples of two problems (society's or personal) that you would consider to be of high magnitude.

    _____

    _____

11. Give an example of a time when informal diction would be appropriate and a time when formal diction would be required.

    _____

    _____

12. List five numbers related to an area of your life (such as test scores, miles walked, or money spent on coffee), and determine the mean for them. Example: miles Jo walked each day for five days: 1, 4, 3, 7, and 5. The mean is 4 miles.

    _____

Crossword Puzzle

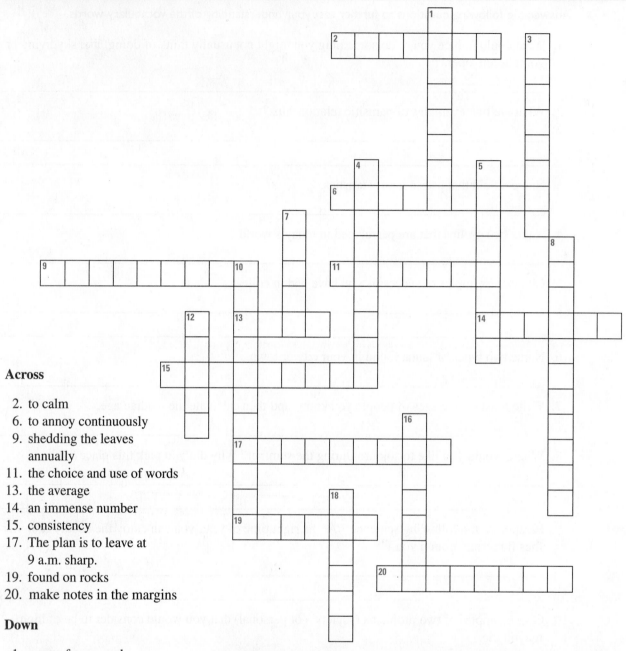

Across

2. to calm
6. to annoy continuously
9. shedding the leaves annually
11. the choice and use of words
13. the average
14. an immense number
15. consistency
17. The plan is to leave at 9 a.m. sharp.
19. found on rocks
20. make notes in the margins

Down

1. x or y, for example
3. a likeness
4. poor
5. living on one's own
7. an allotment
8. having conflicting feelings
10. balanced
12. the plants of a given region taken as a whole
16. a trip to the beach for the weekend
18. That isn't the way it happened.

Use the following words to complete the crossword puzzle. You will use each word once.

VOCABULARY LIST

ambivalence	annotate	autonomy	coherence
deciduous	destitute	diction	flora
intention	lichen	mean	myriad
parallel	persecute	placate	quota
refute	sojourn	symmetrical	variable

Mix It Up

Making a Scene

Get together with six to nine classmates and divide into two to three groups. Each group creates a situation or uses one of the suggestions below to write a short scene using at least six of the vocabulary words to be studied. If you want to study several words, make sure each group doesn't pick the same six words. Each group acts out the scene with the rest noting how the words are used. You may choose to emphasize the vocabulary word by your actions or tone of voice when you are doing the scene to help you and your classmates remember the word. Discuss how the words fit in after the scene is completed. The scenes can also be done as role-playing with pairs creating the scenes instead of small groups. The scenes might be from the readings, such as two people taking a walk in the woods from Chapter 4. Creating scenes is an especially fun and useful activity if you like to act or enjoy movement.

The following are possible scenes related to specific chapters: immigrants sharing their reasons for coming to the United States from Chapter 1, students in a writing circle evaluating a paper from Chapter 2, a teacher and students discussing the homework from Chapter 3, and a ranger leading a group on a hike from Chapter 4.

If you enjoy this collaborative activity, remember to use it again when you are reviewing later chapters in this book. Have fun making the scenes, and you will enjoy the review process.

The Importance of Hello

Greetings are a **socialization** behavior that most people take for granted because greetings are so **pervasive** in society. But from a young age, people are taught the appropriate greetings for different circumstances.

5 Studying everyday life can help us better understand why we act the ways we do. Sociologist Erving Goffman points out that greetings are part of our face-to-face contacts, phone conversations, and letters.

One area that greetings illuminate is **status**. For
10 example, which person says "hello" first and how someone is greeted can be part of the **stratification** system in a society. In the past, a man removed his hat and bowed to greet a prince or king; this behavior showed his lower rank in the society. This greeting be-
15 came truncated over time. Later, people began to greet equals by just lifting the hat and then by touching the hat. Finally, a motion toward the hat was enough of a greeting among friends.

Greetings also show cultural differences. In France,
20 people kiss each other on the cheeks as a friendly, everyday greeting, but this type of behavior is not the **norm** in the United States. In fact, activities that are acceptable in one country may seem odd or even be **taboo** in another country. Learning what is acceptable and what is prohibited is important for travelers, especially for those conducting international business. In the United Sates, most business introductions
25 begin with a firm, short (three- to four-second) handshake. In Europe, business associates also shake hands, but the handshake is usually more formal. Business greetings in Europe rarely display the friendly backslaps that are sometimes seen in the United States. In Japan, people customarily bow as a greeting, and many business people have learned to look carefully at how the bow is done. The depth of a bow reflects the status between the two people. In Arab countries, men often greet each other with a hand on
30 the right shoulder and a kiss on each cheek. Though a handshake is usually used when meeting people from other regions, it may be done with two hands and be more of a handhold. In Latin American countries, male friends hug each other when they meet, and women kiss each other on the cheeks. In business settings, the handshake is typically the norm at first; however, after a third or fourth meeting, a hug might be given. Visitors are generally allowed some flexibility in greeting ceremonies, but because greetings are
35 so ingrained, a native of a country may be **ostracized** if he or she fails to follow proper behavior.

Linguist C. A. Ferguson, as an informal experiment, decided to **deviate** from **conventional** greeting behavior at work. For two days in a row, he didn't respond to his secretary's "good morning." He reported that the atmosphere was unpleasant on the first day and tense on the second day. By the third day, to **alleviate** the stress and save their working relationship, he discontinued the experiment. What people
40 say and do in what may seem like simple greetings can have more importance than people imagine.

Predicting ||||||||||||||||||||||||||||||||||||||||||||||||||||||||||||||||||||||||||||||

For each set, write the definition on the line next to the word to which it belongs. If you are unsure, return to the reading on page 44, and underline any context clues you find. After you've made your predictions, check your answers against the Word List on page 49. Place a checkmark in the box next to each word whose definition you missed. These are the words you'll want to study closely.

Set One

> standing, especially social standing   a standard   the act of developing levels of class
>
> a learning process   having the quality to spread throughout

- ❑ 1. **socialization** (line 1) _____
- ❑ 2. **pervasive** (line 2) _____
- ❑ 3. **status** (line 9) _____
- ❑ 4. **stratification** (line 11) _____
- ❑ 5. **norm** (line 22) _____

Set Two

> excluded   to relieve   forbidden from use   to move away from a set behavior   customary

- ❑ 6. **taboo** (line 23) _____
- ❑ 7. **ostracized** (line 35) _____
- ❑ 8. **deviate** (line 36) _____
- ❑ 9. **conventional** (line 36) _____
- ❑ 10. **alleviate** (line 39) _____

Self-Tests ||||||||||||||||||||||||||||||||||||||||||||||||||||||||||||||||||||||||||||||||||||||

1 Put a T for true or F for false next to each statement.

_____ 1. A group might consider ostracizing someone with an unpleasant odor.

_____ 2. Ox-drawn carts are pervasive in American society.

_____ 3. A massage can help to alleviate stress.

_____ 4. One's status in society is often determined by one's job.

_____ 5. Spending the weekend skiing in Switzerland is the norm for most students.

_____ 6. Riding a pogo stick is a conventional method of transportation.

_____ 7. Blowing bubbles with one's gum is considered taboo in the classroom.

_____ 8. There is no type of stratification in the military.

_____ 9. A flooded road can cause people to deviate from an intended route.

_____ 10. Socialization can take place at the dinner table.

2 Finish the reading using the vocabulary words. Use each word once.

VOCABULARY LIST

alleviate	norm	pervasive	conventional	socialization
status	taboo	deviate	ostracized	stratification

Fitting In

The years spent in school are certainly an important part of the (1)_____ process. It is during school hours that children learn how to get along with others and how different groups act. Certainly (2)_____ is part of the schoolyard. Some students are the "in" group and have special privileges, while others are considered "outsiders." One's (3)_____ in school can help determine whether one is invited to parties or teased during recess. Those who (4)_____ from the accepted standards, whether by wearing out-of-style clothes or not keeping up on the latest slang, can expect to be criticized. In extreme cases, these students may even be (5)_____. What is considered right and wrong can change quickly. One week it may be (6)_____ to wear stripes, and the next week stripes can be all the rage.

To (7)_____ the stress of trying to fit in, parents should give their children love and encouragement at home. The need to fit in, however, is (8)_____ in society, so parents should balance accepting some requests for the latest gadgets with giving in to every childhood whim. What was the (9)_____ when parents went to school and what is the standard today can vary greatly, and parents must be willing to change their ideas of what is and isn't acceptable. The (10)_____ wisdom that "father knows best" may not always hold true in a rapidly changing world.

3 Circle the word that best completes each sentence.

1. Instead of using the (conventional, pervasive) entrance, my brother likes to enter the house through his bedroom window.

2. To (deviate, alleviate) the pain, Elizabeth put ice on her sore knee.

3. I kept asking about the (norm, status) of the flight, but no one at the check-in counter was sure when the plane would take off.

4. It is usually considered (taboo, norm) to ask how much money a person makes.

5. When no one got a raise, discontent was the (conventional, pervasive) mood in the office.

6. I enrolled my son in preschool to help his (socialization, stratification).

7. We had to (deviate, alleviate) from the syllabus because it was worthwhile to attend the assembly.

8. In some countries, such as India, (stratification, taboo) has been very important to how people are treated.

9. It is considered the (norm, taboo) to tip waiters in the United States, but that is not the custom in all countries.

10. Sarah was (ostracized, alleviated) from the cooking club when she brought in a peanut butter and jelly sandwich and called it gourmet food.

Word Wise

Collocations

The *conventional wisdom* has been that eating dessert will make a person fat, but it is more likely the portion size and type of dessert that will put on the pounds. (Chapter 7)

We had to *deviate from* the plan when Michelle called in sick since we only had three people to give the presentation instead of four. (Chapter 7)

The *socialization process* starts early with children learning what actions are and are not acceptable in their family. (Chapter 7)

Connotations and Denotations

Conventional (Chapter 7): denotation—"conforming to established standards." For some people the connotation of *conventional* is "boring." They think that "conforming to established standards" is old-fashioned, and they would rather try something new or different. When you hear the word *conventional,* how do you react?

Interesting Etymologies

Ostracize (Chapter 7): comes from the Greek *ostrakon,* "tile or pottery." In ancient Greece when a city wanted to see if a person should be forced to leave because he was in trouble with the state, a vote was taken on tiles. If six thousand people voted "yes," the person was banished for a minimum of five years. Today ostracize has the same effect—"to exclude, by general consent, from society or from privileges"—but without the voting tiles.

Taboo (Chapter 7): comes from the Tongan word *tabu,* "marked as holy." Tongan is a Polynesian language spoken in the Tonga island group, which is located in the southern Pacific Ocean. Taboos were originally restrictions against mentioning certain matters in fear that they might anger the gods. The word came to mean "forbidden from use or mention" or "a prohibition excluding something from use." What is considered taboo changes depending on the society and the time period.

Interactive Exercise ||||||||||||||||||||||||||||||||||||||||||||||||||||||||||||||||||||||||||||||||||||||

Give two examples for each of the following.

1. Where can you see socialization taking place?

   _____   _____

2. What are pervasive problems in today's society?

   _____   _____

3. What jobs have a high status in American society?

   _____   _____

4. What institutions use stratification?

   _____   _____

5. What situations might cause someone to deviate from his or her regular behavior?

   _____   _____

6. What norms are found in the classroom?

   _____   _____

7. What topics are usually considered taboo at dinner parties?

   _____   _____

8. Why might someone be ostracized from a group?

   _____   _____

9. What are conventional Mother's or Father's Day gifts?

   _____   _____

10. What do you do to alleviate pain when you are sick?

   _____   _____

HINT

Finding a Place and Time to Study

To concentrate on what you are studying, you need to find the right environment for you. Because most people concentrate better in a quiet space, turn off the television and radio to see if you can better focus on your work. Also look for a place with good light; you don't want to strain your eyes. You should be comfortable, so find a chair you like, or if you need to take notes, sit at a table. For some people, sitting outside in a park or the back yard provides a pleasant and productive place to read. See what works best for you depending on what you are studying. Change your environment if you can't focus. To further make your studying effective, find the time of day that you are most productive. Decide whether you are a morning, afternoon, or night person. Don't try to get up early to study if you won't really be awake at that time. Or don't stay up late trying to read if all you want to do is close your eyes. Understand how your body works by paying attention to the times of the day when you feel the most tired and the most alert. Your study routine will be improved if you pay attention to your body clock.

Word List

alleviate
[ə lē′ vē āt′]

v. to relieve; to reduce

conventional
[kən ven′ shən əl]

adj. 1. customary
2. conforming to established standards

deviate
[dē′ vē āt′]

v. 1. to move away from a norm or set behavior
2. to cause to turn aside or to differ

norm
[nôrm]

n. a standard or pattern regarded as typical for a specific group

ostracize
[os′ trə sīz′]

v. to exclude, by general consent, from society or from privileges

pervasive
[pər vā′ siv, -ziv]

adj. having the quality to spread throughout; extensive

socialization
[so′ shə li zā′ shən]

n. the process whereby an individual learns the values and behaviors appropriate to his or her culture and status

status
[stā′ təs, stat′ əs]

n. 1. a relative position; standing, especially social standing
2. high standing
3. situation

stratification
[strat′ ə fi kā′ shən]

n. the act or process of developing levels of class or privilege

taboo
[tə bōō′, ta-]

adj. forbidden from use or mention
n. a prohibition excluding something from use
v. to forbid or prohibit

Words to Watch ||||||||||||||||||||||||||||||||||||||||||||||||||||||||||||||||||||||||

Which words would you like to practice with a bit more? Pick 3–5 words to study, and list them below. Write the word and its definition, and compose your own sentence using the word correctly. This extra practice could be the final touch to learning a word.

	Word	Definition	Your Sentence
1.	_____	_____	_____
2.	_____	_____	_____
3.	_____	_____	_____
4.	_____	_____	_____
5.	_____	_____	_____

Music

Changing Sounds

Welcome to tonight's event! The Rolling Rock Show is designed to share fifty years of rock history in one night with more than twenty performers on stage playing the songs you love.

5   Since its **inception** in the 1950s, rock 'n' roll has stirred controversy. Elvis Presley and his swiveling hips startled many conservative Americans. They referred to rock 'n' roll as a **cacophony** and **censured** its being played on the radio or sold in record stores. But the

10 "noise" could not be stopped or the movement quieted. Over the next few years, rock 'n' roll continued to break down the **decorum** of the young as crowds of women chased after the Beatles, screamed through their songs, and fainted at their concerts. During the 1960s, the young

15 **clamored** for even more energetic music. The **execution** of rock music continued to change as rock venues grew. Performers learned to **modulate** their voices and performances depending on whether they were singing in front of thousands at a concert like Woodstock or before an

20 intimate group at a folk café. Performers like Jimi Hendrix and Janis Joplin showed how instruments and voices could be used in dynamic ways.

    The complaints against rock music seemed barely **audible** by the mid-1970s, when punk rock and the Sex

25 Pistols broke the peace. High energy was again vital to the music scene, and poor **acoustics**, found in many of the small halls punk bands first played in, hardly seemed to matter to audiences that spent the night pogoing and slam dancing. Music continued to evolve, and the 1980s and

30 '90s embraced a variety of styles including new wave, hip-hop, and rap. For many performers today, it isn't unusual for their **repertoire** to include a classic song (like "Heatwave") from one of the '60s girl groups to a heavy metal–inspired number.

35   Tonight's concert brings artists together from the 1950s to the present to perform songs from some of their most popular albums as well as works by other rock greats. Enjoy the fun, the flair, and the flavors of rock 'n' roll!

Predicting

For each set, write the definition on the line next to the word to which it belongs. If you are unsure, return to the reading on page 50, and underline any context clues you find. After you've made your predictions, check your answers against the Word List on page 55. Place a checkmark in the box next to each word whose definition you missed. These are the words you'll want to study closely.

Set One

| a harsh sound | dignified conduct | the act of beginning | stated noisily | criticized in a harsh manner |

❑ 1. **inception** (line 5) _____

❑ 2. **cacophony** (line 8) _____

❑ 3. **censured** (line 8) _____

❑ 4. **decorum** (line 12) _____

❑ 5. **clamored** (line 15) _____

Set Two

| all the works that a performer is prepared to present | a style of performance | to adjust |
| the features of a room that determine the quality of sounds in it | | capable of being heard |

❑ 6. **execution** (line 15) _____

❑ 7. **modulate** (line 17) _____

❑ 8. **audible** (line 24) _____

❑ 9. **acoustics** (line 26) _____

❑ 10. **repertoire** (line 32) _____

Self-Tests

1 Circle the word that best completes each sentence.

1. The (cacophony, acoustics) in the concert hall were so good I could hear the characters when they whispered.

2. The performer's (execution, repertoire) surprised me. Not only could he sing and dance, but he could do magic and tell jokes.

3. The soft voice on the phone was scarcely (audible, modulate), but I thought it was my three-year-old niece who answered.

4. The gymnast's (clamor, execution) on the balance beam was flawless.

5. As the clapping increased or decreased, the candidate knew just how to (modulate, censure) her voice for the best effect.

6. At its (inception, repertoire), the mural looked like it would conform to government policies, but people were amazed by the completed piece when the artist dared to put the president's head on the body of a pig.

7. The executive board voted to (modulate, censure) the treasurer for failing to keep receipts for all of his expenses last year.

8. The crowd (clamored, censured) for an encore, and the band obliged by playing three more songs.

9. The (decorum, execution) at the luncheon was disturbed when the waiter dropped a tray of sandwiches in the lap of noble Lady Windermere, thus causing the other women to giggle.

10. Someone had played with my radio, and I awoke to a (decorum, cacophony) of static, which upset my morning.

2 Finish the readings. Use each word once.

Set One

VOCABULARY LIST

acoustics	audible	repertoire	clamor	cacophony

I was disappointed by the concert. First, the (1)_____ were so bad I couldn't hear the music. Then the management fiddled with the sound system, and the (2)_____ that emitted from the speakers caused the audience to cover its ears. Finally, even when the music was (3)_____ and not terrifying, we still weren't pleased. The new problem was the band's (4)_____. It turned out they had only five original songs, and they kept playing them over and over. The audience raised such a(n) (5)_____ about the poor quality of the whole evening that the owners eventually gave us back our money.

Set Two

VOCABULARY LIST

censure	modulate	execution	inception	decorum

At the (6)_____ of rehearsals, the director told the singer to be bold in her performance of the gypsy. He said that (7)_____ was not appropriate. She was supposed to be a wild gypsy; dignified behavior did not fit the role. As rehearsals continued, the director told her that he did not mean to (8)_____ her whole performance, just the scene where she faces her lover's betrayal. She needed to (9)_____ her voice from soft and sad to an almost wild scream. Her (10)_____ of the piece would help to define her character's actions later in the opera.

3 For each set, write the letter of the most logical analogy. See Completing Analogies on page 4 for instructions and practice.

Set One

_____ 1. modulate : voice ::   a. decorum : rudeness

_____ 2. lecture : classroom ::   b. sprain : ankle

_____ 3. inception : start ::   c. execution : boring

_____ 4. early : late ::   d. shy : modest

_____ 5. taste : salty ::   e. censure : Senate meeting

Set Two

_____ 6. audible : silent ::   f. difficult : hard

_____ 7. fire : burns ::   g. brave : cowardly

_____ 8. water : pool ::   h. a car crash : cacophony

_____ 9. clamor : noise ::   i. book : chapters

_____ 10. pianist : repertoire :: j. acoustics : auditorium

Word Wise

Context Clue Mini-Lesson 3

This lesson uses examples to explain the unknown word. The examples may consist of one illustration of the word or be a list of items. In the paragraph below, circle the examples you find that clarify the meaning of the underlined words. Then use the examples to write your own definitions on the lines next to the words that follow the paragraph.

Lucelia had always been a steadfast friend. She came to visit me daily when I was in the hospital, and she wrote to me weekly when I lived overseas for a year. She had also always been easy to talk to and quite vociferous in her opinions. She never hesitated to tell me what brand to buy or who to vote for. I was, therefore, shocked when she came over one night and refused to say anything. She just sat on my couch trembling. I tried to elicit a response by asking her questions like "Are you sick?" or "Do you want a cup of tea?" After an hour, she opened up and told me that she had seen an apparition. She had seen her dead grandmother before and that hadn't seemed to bother her much. This time she said she had seen Napoleon, and seeing a famous person had really scared her.

Your Definition

1. Steadfast _____

2. Vociferous _____

3. Elicit _____

4. Apparition _____

Interactive Exercise

Write your own program notes. Pick a type of music or a performer, and let the audience know what to expect from the show. Include at least seven of the vocabulary words in your write-up.

Some styles of music to choose from:

Rock   Country & Western   Rap   Blues   Hip-Hop   Alternative   Classical   Jazz

_____

_____

_____

_____

_____

_____

_____

_____

_____

_____

_____

_____

HINT

Shades of Meaning

Learning new vocabulary is more than learning synonyms. While some words you learn may be similar to other words you know and may be used in place of another word, every word is unique. Good writers choose their words carefully. Words have different shades of meaning, and conscientious writers think about those differences when picking a word to use. A careful reader also responds to those differences in meaning. In some cases the differences are slight, such as "On Sundays I eat a big dinner" or "On Sundays I eat a large dinner." But replacing "big" or "large" with "huge" or "gigantic" (both synonyms for "big") does alter the image of how much food the person is eating. Some synonyms have even bigger differences. For the sentence, "The clever woman found a way to get out of debt," "clever" could be replaced with the synonyms "smart" or "crafty." The reader would have a different reaction to the woman depending on whether the writer selected "smart" or "crafty." When reading or writing, pay attention to the diverse ways words can be used.

Word List

acoustics
[ə kōō′ stiks]
n. the features of a room or auditorium that determine the quality of the sounds in it

audible
[ô′ də bəl]
adj. capable of being heard; loud enough to hear

cacophony
[kə kof′ ə nē]
n. a harsh, jarring sound

censure
[sen′ shər]
v. to criticize in a harsh manner
n. 1. a strong expression of disapproval
2. an official reprimand

clamor
[klam′ ər]
v. to state noisily
n. a loud uproar; a loud and continued noise

decorum
[di kôr′ əm, -kōr′-]
n. dignified conduct or appearance

execution
[ek′ si kyōō′ shən]
n. 1. a style of performance; technical skill, as in music
2. the act of doing or performing
3. the use of capital punishment

inception
[in sep′ shən]
n. the act of beginning; a start

modulate
[moj′ ə lāt′]
v. to alter (the voice) according to circumstances; to adjust

repertoire
[rep′ ər twär′, -twôr′, rep′ ə-]
n. 1. all the works that a performer is prepared to present
2. the skills used in a particular occupation

Words to Watch

Which words would you like to practice with a bit more? Pick 3–5 words to study, and list them below. Write the word and its definition, and compose your own sentence using the word correctly. This extra practice could be the final touch to learning a word.

Word	Definition	Your Sentence
1. _____	_____	_____
2. _____	_____	_____
3. _____	_____	_____
4. _____	_____	_____
5. _____	_____	_____

9 Foreign Languages

Welcome Additions

More foreign words and phrases come into common English usage each year. Because English has always borrowed words from other languages, people aren't always aware that a word

5 originated in another place. For example, *banana* and *zombie* are African words, *cookie* and *yacht* come from the Dutch, and *yogurt* from Turkish. Other words may still sound foreign, but they are used every day when speaking English.

10   Imagine eating dinner **alfresco** on a pleasant evening. While you are enjoying the view from the patio, your waiter comes to tell you about the soup **du jour** and other daily specials. After you take a sip of the delicious French onion soup you ordered, you sit back and enjoy the **bon mot** your companion credits to Mark Twain: "I am opposed to

15 millionaires, but it would be dangerous to offer me the position." You laugh at the witty remark and then ask, "Who needs to be a millionaire?" You know you are living **la dolce vita** as you take pleasure in your excellent meal, good company, and lovely atmosphere. When your dessert arrives, the waiter lights a match, applies it to the banana flambé, and shouts, "**Voilà!**" The alcohol ignites, and the flames create a magnificent finale to your evening. Possibly without even being aware of it, you have

20 just spent an evening filled with foreign phrases.

    Foreign words also appear frequently in the media. The Latin phrase **carpe diem** was an important message in the 1989 Oscar-winning film *Dead Poet's Society*. The film is about a strict boys' school where an English professor tries to teach his students to live life to the fullest. Carpe diem also appears on numerous calendars and motivational posters.

25 To seize the day is a message we often forget in today's hectic world. The term **doppelgänger** comes from German for a ghostly double, and the concept has been explored in short stories by writers such as Edgar Allan Poe in "William Wilson" and by

30 Robert Louis Stevenson in "Markheim." Writers have also claimed to have seen their doppelgängers. The English poet Shelly saw his shortly before he drowned in Italy, while the German poet Goethe claimed to have seen his riding down a

35 road. Even a single word can have an impact in a story, such as **nada** as used in "A Clean Well-Lighted Place" by Ernest Hemingway. Nothing can certainly come to mean something.

    It isn't necessarily a **faux pas** to not understand every foreign word or phrase currently in use, but to avoid possibly embarrassing moments, the wise person will want to learn at least a few of these phrases.

40 The multicultural **zeitgeist** of the twenty-first century asks all of us to grow along with the language.

Predicting |||||||||||||||||||||||||||||||||||||||||||||||||||||||||||||||||||||||||||||||||||||||||||||||||||||||||||

For each set, write the definition on the line next to the word to which it belongs. If you are unsure, return to the reading on page 56, and underline any context clues you find. After you've made your predictions, check your answers against the Word List on page 61. Place a checkmark in the box next to each word whose definition you missed. These are the words you'll want to study closely.

Set One

There it is!	a witty remark	out-of-doors	the good life	as served on a particular day

☐ 1. **alfresco** (line 10) _____

☐ 2. **du jour** (line 13) _____

☐ 3. **bon mot** (line 14) _____

☐ 4. **la dolce vita** (line 16) _____

☐ 5. **voilà** (line 18) _____

Set Two

nothing	the spirit of the time	seize the day	a mistake	a ghostly double or counterpart

☐ 6. **carpe diem** (line 21) _____

☐ 7. **doppelgänger** (line 28) _____

☐ 8. **nada** (line 36) _____

☐ 9. **faux pas** (line 38) _____

☐ 10. **zeitgeist** (line 40) _____

Self-Tests ||||||||||||||||||||||||||||||||||||||||||||||||||||||||||||||||||||||||||||||||||||||||||||||||||||||

1 Match each word with its synonym in Set One and its antonym in Set Two.

SYNONYMS

SET ONE

_____ 1. carpe diem   a. mood

_____ 2. doppelgänger   b. mistake

_____ 3. bon mot   c. grab the chance

_____ 4. zeitgeist   d. double

_____ 5. faux pas   e. witticism

ANTONYMS
SET TWO

_____ 6. alfresco   f. old

_____ 7. nada   g. Darn!

_____ 8. la dolce vita   h. indoors

_____ 9. voilà   i. everything

_____ 10. du jour   j. dullness

2 Finish the sentences using the vocabulary words. Use each word once.

> **VOCABULARY LIST**
>
> | bon mot | nada | alfresco | dolce vita | doppelgänger |
> |---|---|---|---|---|
> | carpe diem | voilà | faux pas | zeitgeist | du jour |

1. The special _____ at the cafeteria was kidney pie; I decided to pass.

2. As we sat on the porch of our cabin overlooking the lake, we thought this was the _____.

3. Shortly before her death, Queen Elizabeth I is reported to have seen her _____ lying on a bed.

4. My cousin is the expert at the _____; she always knows the right thing to say to make people laugh.

5. After a busy semester, I was looking forward to doing _____ for a week.

6. Sometimes I get so involved in everything I need to get done that I forget to _____.

7. I think that having toilet paper stuck to one's shoe all night would be considered a(n) _____ at most parties.

8. In the 1920s, the _____ seemed to be to party as much as possible in order to forget World War I.

9. The play will be performed _____ to enhance the play's forest setting.

10. I kept trying, and, _____, my story was finally accepted for publication.

3 Connect the vocabulary words to the following items or situations. Use each word once.

VOCABULARY LIST

alfresco	carpe diem	du jour	doppelgänger	voilà
bon mot	faux pas	la dolce vita	nada	zeitgeist

1. a pocket without any lira, pesos, or francs _____
2. French onion soup on Wednesdays _____
3. greed in the 1980s _____
4. under the stars _____
5. "There is only one thing in the world worse than being talked about, and that is not being talked about."—Oscar Wilde _____
6. I found my keys! _____
7. asking a woman whether her child is her grandchild _____
8. When the woman he has admired all semester asks to borrow a pen, the young man asks her out. _____
9. Robert Louis Stevenson's character Markheim meets his evil self. _____
10. a three-course lunch followed by a nap _____

Word Wise

Collocations

The kids *clamored for* more juice; they were thirsty after playing in the park. (Chapter 8)

I like to eat out on Fridays because the *soup du jour* is usually clam chowder—my favorite. (Chapter 9)

Word Pairs

Audible/Inaudible: Audible (Chapter 8) means "capable of being heard." Inaudible means "incapable of being heard." The music from the rock concert was audible ten blocks away. Tammy's voice was inaudible a foot away from me because the music was so loud.

Interesting Etymologies

Doppelgänger (Chapter 9): comes from the German *doppel,* "double" and *gänger,* "goer or walker." The meaning of doppelgänger is "a ghostly double or counterpart of a living person." There is a theory that a person's double is somewhere out there. There is also the belief that a person will die soon after seeing his or her doppelgänger. Famous people from Catherine the Great to Goethe have reported seeing their doppelgänger. The doppelgänger theme is popular in literature and film from Guy de Maupassant's short story "Lui" to the film *The Man with My Face.*

Interactive Exercise

Write a sentence that provides an example for each word. Try to relate the example to your life or your community to better help you remember the word. For some of the words, your examples may need to be fictitious.

Examples:

dolce vita <u>A lot of people in my community consider la dolce vita to be sailing on one of the nearby lakes on a sunny day.</u>

doppelgänger <u>My husband and I met a clerk at a hotel who could have been the doppelgänger for my sister-in-law. We both thought she looked and sounded just like Terri.</u>

1. alfresco _____
2. carpe diem _____
3. doppelgänger _____
4. faux pas _____
5. voilà _____
6. bon mot _____
7. zeitgeist _____
8. dolce vita _____
9. du jour _____
10. nada _____

Word Part Reminder

Below are a few short exercises to help you review the word parts you have been learning. Fill in the missing word part from the list, and circle the meaning of the word part found in each sentence. Try to complete the questions without returning to the Word Parts chapter, but if you get stuck, look back at Chapter 5.

Example: My daughter needs to learn that the proper place (to put) her trash is in the garbage can; she thinks it is all right to dis*pos*e of it on the floor of her room.

lev   vi   dom   mag

1. Darlene always makes a problem greater than it is; I get tired of the way she has to _____nify everything to make herself important.

2. For my brother, living the good life means a sixty-mile bike ride followed by a carton of chocolate ice cream, but for me la dolce _____ta is a hike in the woods and a big bowl of cherries.

3. I was so impressed when the magician made the woman rise four feet into the air. I had never seen a person _____itate before.

4. I can't imagine a worse condition than living in a country where people don't have any free_____s.

Word List

alfresco
[al fres′ kō]
Italian   *adv.* out-of-doors; in the open air
  adj. outdoor

bon mot
[bôn mō′]
French   *n.* a witty remark or comment; witticism

carpe diem
[kär′ pe dē′ em, kär′ pä dē′ əm]
Latin   *n.* seize the day; enjoy the present

dolce vita
[dōl′ chä vē′ tä]
Italian   *n.* the good life (usually preceded by *la*)

doppelgänger
[dop′ əl gäng′ ər]
German   *n.* a ghostly double or counterpart of a living person

du jour
[də zhoor′, dōō-]
French   *adj.* 1. as prepared or served on a particular day
  2. fashionable; current

faux pas
[fō pä′]
French   *n.* a mistake; a slip or blunder in manners or conduct; an embarrassing social error

nada
[nä′ dä]
Spanish   *n.* nothing

voilà
[vwä lä′]
French   *interj.* There it is! (used to express success or satisfaction)

zeitgeist
[tsīt′ gīst′, zīt′]
German   *n.* the spirit of the time; the general feeling of a particular period of time

Words to Watch

Which words would you like to practice with a bit more? Pick 3–5 words to study, and list them below. Write the word and its definition, and compose your own sentence using the word correctly. This extra practice could be the final touch to learning a word.

	Word	Definition	Your Sentence
1.			
2.			
3.			
4.			
5.			

10

Geography

The Frozen Continent

Antarctica has fascinated people for centuries. The **terrain** includes tall mountains, active volcanoes, and valleys of rock that are surprisingly clear of any ice or snow. It also contains the largest mass of ice in the
5 world. The continent and the surrounding oceans contain more than 90% of the world's ice and 75% of its fresh water. Considering the area's cold temperatures, the abundance of ice is understandable. Temperatures **fluctuate** on the continent depending on the time of
10 year and location. The record low for Antarctica is −128.5° F (−89.2° C) at Vostock Station on the polar **plateau**. The average temperature at the South Pole is −59.8° F (−51° C). The Antarctica **Peninsula** is con-

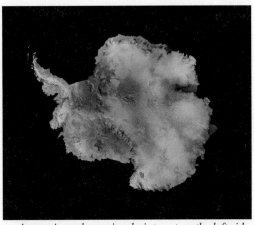

Antarctica—the peninsula juts out on the left side.

siderably warmer than the interior. During the winter, temperatures average 4° F (−20° C), and in the
15 summer, temperatures get just above freezing, or around 35–40° F (2–4° C). Despite the ice, Antarctica is one of the driest places on Earth. The interior of the continent is considered a polar desert because it gets no rain and little snow. The peninsula gets more snow and some rain in the summer.

For the last two hundred years, whalers, explorers, and scientists have made Antarctica home for short periods of time. Whalers were active from the early 1900s to the 1960s. Serious scientific explo-
20 ration of Antarctica began in the 1800s. Extreme **fortitude** was needed to be an explorer in the early days, as clothing was not always as warm as was needed and transportation was difficult. Dogs and ponies were used to pull sleds, and at times the men were forced to pull their heavily laden sleds themselves. Among the **escapades** of the early explorers was a race to be the first to reach the South Pole. In 1911, Roald Amundsen of Norway and Robert Scott of Britain each undertook to reach the pole. Amundsen was the
25 first to arrive on December 14, 1911. Scott's party arrived thirty-three days later to find the Norwegian flag and a tent left by Amundsen. Scott's **expedition** had been filled with problems, which worsened on the return. Titus Oates was suffering from frost-bitten feet. Fearing he was slowing the team, one night during a blizzard, he told the other men, "I am just going outside and may be some time." His **magnanimous** gesture was in vain. Strong storms continued, and in a few days, the rest of the group per-
30 ished within eleven miles of the next supply station.

In the late 1950s, scientists saw the need to protect the **pristine** environment of Antarctica. Several nations (including Chile, Argentina, the United States, the Soviet Union, and Britain) cooperated to create the Antarctic
35 Treaty. Every nation that signs the treaty agrees to protect the flora and fauna and to consider the environmental impact of any actions in the area. Today the population of Antarctica **burgeons** in the summer with several countries reopening their research stations after the harsh win-
40 ter. Among the goals of these stations are to learn more about the plants and animals of this last great frontier and to preserve the unspoiled continent.

Predicting

For each set, write the definition on the line next to the word to which it belongs. If you are unsure, return to the reading on page 62, and underline any context clues you find. After you've made your predictions, check your answers against the Word List on page 67. Place a checkmark in the box next to each word whose definition you missed. These are the words you'll want to study closely.

Set One

> mental and emotional strength   an area of land   an area of land almost fully surrounded by water
>
> a land area having a fairly level surface elevated above adjoining land   to vary irregularly

❑ 1. **terrain** (line 2) _____

❑ 2. **fluctuate** (line 9) _____

❑ 3. **plateau** (line 12) _____

❑ 4. **peninsula** (line 13) _____

❑ 5. **fortitude** (line 20) _____

Set Two

> adventures   unspoiled   a journey   grows   unselfish

❑ 6. **escapades** (line 23) _____

❑ 7. **expedition** (line 26) _____

❑ 8. **magnanimous** (line 29) _____

❑ 9. **pristine** (line 32) _____

❑ 10. **burgeons** (line 38) _____

Self-Tests

1 Put a T for true or F for false next to each statement.

_____ 1. If the price of bread stays the same for ten years, it can be said to fluctuate.

_____ 2. Giving a fellow student a ride home after his car breaks down even though it is fifteen miles out of your way would be a magnanimous gesture.

_____ 3. A person needs fortitude to run a marathon.

_____ 4. One could swim all the way around a peninsula.

_____ 5. An expedition into the depths of a cave requires special gear.

_____ 6. A terrain filled with boulders would be easy to ride a bike on.

_____ 7. The city dump could be considered a pristine area.

_____ 8. Driving across the United States with only $80 in your pocket and no credit cards or other source of money could be considered an escapade.

_____ 9. A plant left in a dark room will likely burgeon.

_____ 10. Mount Everest would be considered a plateau.

2 Finish the journal entries using the vocabulary words. Use each word once.

Set One

VOCABULARY LIST

fluctuated	pristine	terrain	fortitude	expedition

January 16, 1914

We are preparing to leave the area. I am going to miss it here. Though the (1)_____ is covered with snow and the temperatures have been below freezing, it is a beautiful place. The (2)_____ nature of Antarctica attracts me. Everything is so pure and untouched by humans. The (3)_____ has been a success. We have done much research and made some fascinating discoveries. My (4)_____ has been tested by the whole journey, and I am proud to say that I have had the power to withstand the hardships. My interest in exploration has (5)_____ over the years, but this expedition has reignited a desire to see the world and its many fascinating geographic features.

Set Two

VOCABULARY LIST

magnanimous	escapade	plateau	peninsula	burgeoned

November 20, 1921

We have made it to the (6)_____, and it is a pleasure to see water again. The interior was much harsher than this area, and the climb up the (7)_____ exhausted me, especially since I had to take turns pulling our gear in the sled. Ernest has been quite (8)_____ and taken much longer pulls than I have. Tonight we rested and enjoyed watching the penguins. I thought I would be cursing myself for attempting this (9)_____, but I have done quite well. My confidence has (10)_____ as I have successfully dealt with each difficulty we have met on this expedition.

3 Match each example to the vocabulary word it best fits. Use each word once.

1. company earnings unchanged for three years _____
2. preparing oneself to speak in front of a crowd _____
3. an unexplored ice cave _____
4. a trek into the Amazon jungle _____
5. Monday's high 95 degrees, Tuesday's 58, and Wednesday's 79 _____
6. the Kenai in Alaska, Yucatan in Mexico, or Jutland in Denmark _____
7. going to the doughnut shop during a blizzard _____
8. filled with boulders _____
9. wildflowers in the desert after a rainy season _____
10. letting someone else have the last cookie _____

Word Wise

Collocations

I seem to have *reached a plateau* in my weight loss; I have not gained or lost a pound in four weeks. (Chapter 10)

I love to camp in the interior of the park. It is a *pristine environment* because so few people make the effort to hike back here. (Chapter 10)

Interesting Etymologies

Escapade (Chapter 10): comes from the Spanish *escapada,* "a prank, flight, or escape." The root is *escapar,* "to escape." The meaning of "an adventure, especially one contrary to usual or proper behavior" shows elements of flight and escape from conventional rules.

Peninsula (Chapter 10): comes from the Latin *paeninsula,* "almost an island." It is made from *paene,* "almost," plus *insula,* "island." The definition of "an area of land almost fully surrounded by water except for a narrow strip of land connecting it with the mainland" shows its "almost island" status.

Plateau (Chapter 10): comes from the French word *plateau.* In Old French, the root was *platel,* "a flat piece of metal, wood, etc.," which comes from *plat,* "flat surface or thing." The definition of a plateau as "a land area having a fairly level surface elevated above adjoining land" illustrates its "flat surface" origin.

Interactive Exercise

Pretend you are going on an expedition. Pick a place to travel to, consider going to someplace extremely cold or hot to test your fortitude, and write a journal entry describing your adventure. Use at least seven of the vocabulary words in your entry.

_____

_____

_____

_____

_____

_____

_____

_____

_____

_____

_____

_____

_____

Conversation Starters

An excellent way to review the vocabulary words and help to make them your own is to use them when you are speaking. Gather three to five friends or classmates, and use one or more of the conversation starters below. Before you begin talking, have each person write down six of the vocabulary words he or she will use during the conversation. Share your lists with each other to check that you did not all pick the same six words. Try to cover all of the words you want to study, whether you are reviewing one, two, or more chapters.

1. How important are greetings in your interactions with people? How do you greet your friends? Does that differ from how you greet your professors?

2. What types of music do you like? What attracts you to these styles? Is there a type of music you really dislike? Why is that?

3. Do you know a foreign language? Was it hard to learn? If you could learn any foreign language, what would it be? Why did you make this choice?

4. Would you like to travel to Antarctica? Or is there a warmer place you would prefer to visit? Closer to home, what are a couple of interesting places you could make an expedition to within a day's drive of your house? Are there any interesting geographic features at these places?

Word List

burgeon
[bûr′ jən]
v. to flourish; to grow; to sprout

escapade
[es′ kə pād′,
es′ kə pād′]
n. an adventure, especially one contrary to usual or proper behavior

expedition
[ek′ spi dish′ ən]
n. 1. a journey made for a specific purpose, such as exploration
2. the group of persons occupied in such a journey

fluctuate
[fluk′ choo āt′]
v. to vary irregularly; to change

fortitude
[fôr′ ti tood′]
n. mental and emotional strength in bravely facing challenges or danger

magnanimous
[mag nan′ ə məs]
adj. showing a noble spirit; unselfish; generous in forgiving

peninsula
[pə nin′ sə lə]
n. an area of land almost fully surrounded by water except for a narrow strip of land connecting it with the mainland

plateau
[pla tō′]
n. 1. a land area having a fairly level surface elevated above adjoining land; a tableland
2. a period with little or no change; a stable state

pristine
[pris′ tēn,
pri stēn′]
adj. unspoiled; pure; uncorrupted

terrain
[tə rān′]
n. an area of land, especially in reference to its natural features

Words to Watch

Which words would you like to practice with a bit more? Pick 3–5 words to study, and list them below. Write the word and its definition, and compose your own sentence using the word correctly. This extra practice could be the final touch to learning a word.

	Word	Definition	Your Sentence
1.	_____	_____	_____
	_____	_____	_____
2.	_____	_____	_____
	_____	_____	_____
3.	_____	_____	_____
	_____	_____	_____
4.	_____	_____	_____
	_____	_____	_____
5.	_____	_____	_____
	_____	_____	_____

11

Word Parts II

Look for words with these **prefixes, roots,** and/or **suffixes** as you work through this book. You may have already seen some of them, and you will see others in later chapters. Learning basic word parts can help you figure out the meanings of unfamiliar words.

prefix: a word part added to the beginning of a word that changes the meaning of the root

root: a word's basic part with its essential meaning

suffix: a word part added to the end of a word; indicates the part of speech

Word Part	Meaning	Examples and Definitions
Prefixes		
ex-	out, out of, former	*export:* to send or carry goods out of a country *exclude:* to keep out
per-	through, throughout, completely	*pervasive:* spreading throughout *perform:* to go through with; to complete
sym-	with, together	*symbiotic:* pertaining to the living together of two dissimilar organisms *symphony:* brings together a combination of sounds
Roots		
-flu-, -flux-	to flow	*affluence:* a flowing toward *influx:* an act of flowing in
-her-, -hes-	to stick	*coherent:* sticking to one point *adhesive:* sticky
-plac-	to please	*placate:* to please; to calm *placid:* pleasantly calm
-port-	to carry	*portfolio:* a case for carrying papers or drawings *portable:* easy to carry
-sta-, -sti-	to stand, to be in a place	*status:* standing; social position *destitute:* lacking; without support or standing
Suffixes		
-most (makes an adjective)	most	*utmost:* the most extreme *foremost:* the most important
-phobia (makes a noun)	fear of	*acrophobia:* a fear of heights *claustrophobia:* a fear of enclosed places

Self-Tests

1 Read each definition, and choose the appropriate word. Use each word once. The meaning of the word part is underlined to help you make the connection. Refer to the Word Parts list if you need help.

> **VOCABULARY LIST**
>
> | | | | | |
> |---|---|---|---|---|
> | pervade | fluid | foremost | complacent | exhale |
> | sympathize | export | coherent | anthrophobia | stationary |

1. to feel <u>with</u> someone _____
2. <u>pleased</u> with oneself often without an awareness of some problem _____
3. a substance that is capable of <u>flowing</u> _____
4. <u>sticking</u> to one point _____
5. to breathe <u>out</u> _____
6. the <u>most</u> important _____
7. a <u>fear of</u> people _____
8. to <u>carry out of</u> a country _____
9. to spread <u>throughout</u> _____
10. <u>standing</u> still; not moving _____

2 Finish the sentences with the meaning of each word part. Use each meaning once. The word part is underlined to help you make the connection.

> **VOCABULARY LIST**
>
> | | | | | |
> |---|---|---|---|---|
> | please | out of | together | completely | stick |
> | flow | most | stand | fear of | to carry |

1. Claire used <u>ex</u>tortion to get money _____ the man.
2. Her perfume <u>per</u>meated the room; the smell _____ took over the space.
3. Anthony is <u>flu</u>ent in five languages. The ability to speak another language just seems to _____ out of him.
4. I enjoy going to the <u>sym</u>phony. I like how all the instruments come _____ to make beautiful sounds.
5. To <u>plac</u>ate the hungry guests, Jane thought she could _____ them with cheese and crackers before the main course was ready.
6. I did not know Tina suffered from ailuro<u>phobia</u> until Seeley jumped on her lap and she confessed to a _____ cats.
7. The ad<u>hes</u>ive tape really helped my package _____ together. My sister said it took her an hour to get it open.
8. I reveal my inner<u>most</u> secrets to my diary. I don't dare share my _____ secret feelings with anyone.
9. I asked the <u>port</u>er at the train station _____ my bags to my car because I was tired of lifting them.
10. I am not going to let any ob<u>sta</u>cles (financial, emotional, or time-consuming) _____ in the way of my completing college.

3 Finish the story using the word parts found below. Use each word part once. Your knowledge of word parts, as well as the context clues, will help you create the correct words. If you do not understand the meaning of a word you have made, check the dictionary for the definition or to see whether the word exists.

WORD PARTS LIST

her	ex	plac	sti	sym
per	most	flu	port	phobia

Crossing a Bridge

For years I suffered from aqua(1)_____. My
fear of water had been with me since I was a teenager. I
can remember swimming in the community pool when I
was in elementary school, but something happened around
the age of fourteen that led to an intense fear of being in,
on, or over water. I went to a psychologist who suggested
that my fear could be a(n) (2)_____ptom of a
larger problem, but I wasn't willing to explore that idea.

My fear (3)_____cluded my doing so many things. I once had the chance to
im(4)_____ some beautiful vases for my antique shop, but the man in Japan would only sell to
me personally, and I was afraid to fly over the Pacific Ocean. My fear also never (5)_____mitted
me to take hikes in the local woods with the rest of my family because I would have had to cross several
streams. I looked fondly at their photographs for years, and they kept encouraging me to join them. And, of
course, the swimming that I enjoyed as a child was absolutely out of the question.

My son finally forced me to quit being so ob(6)_____nate and face my fear. He
reminded me that I had always ad(7)_____ed to the idea that he could do anything, so he
asked why couldn't I. He took me to a beautiful spot in the woods and showed me how
(8)_____id the water was under the bridge. It certainly did look calm, almost pleasant. Then
he showed me how to walk carefully across the bridge. With a few in(9)_____ential words,
he coaxed me across the bridge. It was a major breakthrough! I was so proud of myself.

After two more years of gradual progress, I am ready to undertake a trip to the
southern(10)_____ point on the planet. I am planning a cruise to Antarctica. I will actually
be spending two weeks on a ship. Now I truly believe fears can be overcome. I wish I hadn't waited
so long to face mine.

4 Pick the best definition for each underlined word using your knowledge of word parts. Circle the word part in each of the underlined words.

a. the maximum

b. conduct; how one carries oneself

c. tending to unify or stick together

d. sweetly or smoothly flowing

e. not to be pacified or pleased

f. cannot be passed through

g. stale or foul from standing, as in a pool of water

h. the former president

i. an abnormal fear of being alone

j. a pleasant arrangement of parts with each other

_____ 1. Because our dog has <u>monophobia</u>, we have to take her with us everywhere.

_____ 2. The bank's new lock is <u>impervious</u> to known methods of safe cracking.

_____ 3. The <u>symmetry</u> of the building made it appealing to most people.

_____ 4. I was proud of my son's <u>deportment</u> at the luncheon. He is usually loud, but he was quiet and well mannered.

_____ 5. The <u>ex-president</u> of the company had to face a barrage of questions from reporters about his actions after it was discovered that he had hidden money in a secret account.

_____ 6. I tried my <u>utmost</u> to keep the party a surprise, but the day before her graduation, I accidently mentioned ordering a cake, and Colleen guessed that there was something going on.

_____ 7. The <u>stagnant</u> pond had a horrible smell to it.

_____ 8. The singer's <u>mellifluous</u> voice kept the audience enchanted for two hours.

_____ 9. Because of the movie's <u>cohesive</u> structure, it was easy to understand how the different characters all came to know each other.

_____ 10. The little boy was <u>implacable</u>; nothing would quiet him until his mother stopped at the toy store.

5 A good way to remember word parts is to pick one word that uses a word part and understand how that word part functions in the word. Then you can apply that meaning to other words that have the same word part. Use the words to help you match the word part to its meaning.

Set One

_____ 1. **ex-:** export, exclude, ex-husband

_____ 2. **-flu-, -flux-:** fluid, fluctuate, influx

_____ 3. **-sta-, -sti-:** status, static, destitute

_____ 4. **-most:** utmost, foremost, southernmost

_____ 5. **-plac-:** placate, placid, complacent

a. to flow

b. to please

c. out, out of, former

d. to stand, to be in a place

e. most

Set Two

_____ 6. **per-:** pervasive, perennial, permutation

_____ 7. **-port-:** portfolio, portable, import

_____ 8. **sym-:** symbiotic, symmetrical, sympathy

_____ 9. **-her-, -hes-:** coherent, inherent, adhesive

_____ 10. **-phobia:** acrophobia, metrophobia, aquaphobia

f. fear of

g. to carry

h. through, throughout, completely

i. with, together

j. to stick

Interactive Exercise ||||||||||||||||||||||||||||||||||||||||||||||||||||||||||||||||||||||||||

Use the dictionary to find a word you don't know that uses each word part listed below. Write the meaning of the word part, the word, and the definition. If your dictionary has the etymology (history) of the word, see how the word part relates to the meaning, and write the etymology after the definition.

Word Part	Meaning	Word	Definition and Etymology
EXAMPLE:			
-flu-	to flow	fluvial	formed by the action of flowing water
			From Latin "fluvius," river; from "fluere," to flow
1. ex-			
2. per-			
3. -port-			
4. -sta-			
5. sym-			

Word Wise

A perfect place to practice your newly acquired vocabulary is on the Internet. You can share your thoughts with others and use new words by writing a book review at amazon.com. This online bookstore has a space for you to write reviews of the books it sells. Go to the site and type in the name of a book you would like to review. You can pick a book you enjoyed reading or one that you disliked. It can be a work of fiction or nonfiction. You may even want to rate one of your textbooks. If Amazon sells the book, it will come up in a list of books. Go to the page for the book you want, and click on the "Write a review" link. You will need to supply an e-mail address and a password before you can begin your review. Click on the "review guidelines" to read Amazon's rules for writing a review. Your review can be from 75 to 300 words. You will be asked to rate the book from 1 to 5 stars, supply a title for your review, and then write the review. Remember to use some of the vocabulary words you are learning in your review. You can use your real name on the review or create a pen name. Read through the directions for both to decide which you want to do. Most reviews are posted within one day. Once your review is posted, let your classmates know what book you reviewed. You can then read each others' reviews and practice reading the vocabulary words in new contexts. Your instructor may ask you to print out your review to display it in class or to read it aloud. Have fun sharing your opinions with the world and getting a chance to use your new knowledge in a real-life setting.

HINT

Test-Taking Strategies

Studying is essential to do well on a test, but for some people that isn't enough to ease the stress that testing can bring. A few strategies may help you deal with test anxiety.

- Get a good night's rest, and eat a healthy breakfast, lunch, or dinner before the exam.
- Exercise before the exam. Take a walk or do some stretching to help you relax.
- When you get to the classroom, take a few deep breaths and visualize yourself in a soothing spot such as hiking in a forest or taking a bath. Also picture yourself as being successful at the test; don't focus on any negatives.
- Read each question carefully. Look for important words in a question such as "the least" or "always."
- If the test is multiple-choice, read each of the choices before making your decision. Be aware of choices such as "all of the above" or "none of the above."
- If the test is a fill-in-the-blank, try putting each choice in the blank and see which sounds best.
- If you get stuck on a question in a matching test, go on to the next one. When you finish answering the questions that are easy for you, see which questions and choices are left. With fewer choices, the answers should be easier to find (for example, look at Self-Tests 2 and 3 in this chapter).

Being a bit nervous can help during a test by keeping you alert, but too much stress can ruin even the most prepared student's chances of success. If text anxiety becomes a serious problem for you, check with the counselors at your college for advice.

Focus on Chapters 7–11

The following activities give you a chance to interact some more with the vocabulary words you've been learning. By looking at art, taking tests, answering questions, doing a crossword puzzle, and working with others, you will see which words you know well and which you still need to work with.

Art

Match each picture below to one of the following vocabulary words. Use each word once.

VOCABULARY LIST

stratification	alfresco	cacophony
peninsula	taboo	plateau

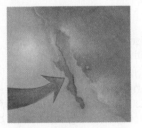

1. _____

2. _____

3. _____

4. _____

5. _____

6. _____

1 Pick the word that best completes each sentence.

1. It was a(n) _____ gesture on my neighbor's part to give me his tickets to the sold-out play after he heard how much I was in love with the lead actor.

   a. du jour   b. audible   c. magnanimous   d. conventional

2. As she read to the children, the teacher _____ her voice from a whisper to a yell depending on what was happening in the story.

   a. modulated   b. alleviated   c. ostracized   d. burgeoned

3. Gerald amused his dinner companions with a _____ about a recent film.

   a. repertoire   b. bon mot   c. status   d. plateau

4. The _____ in the auditorium could be improved: I thought the president of the college said, "Welcome to the graduation cemetery."

   a. expedition   b. acoustics   c. faux pas   d. stratification

5. Methods of _____ differ among cultures; for example, many societies have special initiation ceremonies into adulthood.

   a. terrain   b. doppelganger   c. repertoire   d. socialization

2 Complete the following sentences using the vocabulary words. Use each word once.

a. inception	b. escapade	c. carpe diem	d. status	e. faux pas

1. I'm going to go online and check the _____ of the package I sent yesterday. I have the tracking number, so I can check on its progress across the country.

2. The sun is finally shining. This weekend I'm going to follow the motto _____ and take advantage of the good weather to go camping in the mountains.

3. My mother would have been disappointed in me. She considers it a(n) _____ to not bring the host or hostess of a party a small gift. I meant to buy flowers on the way, but I ran out of time.

4. Since its _____, there have been only disagreements on how to operate the policy.

5. My sister should be sending me an e-mail on my nephew's latest _____. He and his friends are bicycling across the country and having some great adventures.

3 Finish the story using the vocabulary words. Use each word once.

VOCABULARY LIST

burgeoned	audible	deviate	la dolce vita	fluctuated	ostracize
du jour	alleviate	pristine	voilà	repertoire	clamor

Life on a Farm

To (1)_____ the boredom that had set into my life, I decided to live on a farm for a year. My friends tried to convince me that it was not going to be (2)_____ that I had in mind. Most of them who had grown up on farms didn't feel that it would be my definition of the good life, and they cautioned me that things were not often (3)_____.

They were worried because I keep my apartment extremely neat. However, part of the change I was looking forward to was getting dirty.

I headed off to the farm. My enthusiasm (4)_____ when I saw the horses, cows, and ducks. Everything looked so different and peaceful. My excitement (5)_____ several times over the next few weeks. I was not pleased with the (6)_____ sound of roosters at 5 a.m., nor the (7)_____ of pots and pans as the owners of the house began getting breakfast ready at 5:30. I had to learn to (8)_____ from my city schedule of getting up at 8 or 9. But change is what I wanted from this escapade. I grew to enjoy getting up early and finding out what the activity (9)_____ would be. I hadn't realized how large the (10)_____ of a farmer is. He or she has to have a variety of skills, from driving a tractor to milking a cow. I learned to do both. I also learned how to pick fruit, plant a vegetable garden, bake bread, and collect eggs, among other things.

I didn't want to totally (11)_____ myself from my friends, so I invited them to visit a few times. They came for a huge picnic in the summer filled with fruits and vegetables from the farm, and they loved swimming in the nearby lake. They came again in the fall and joined in the apple picking. That's when they admitted that it looked like I was doing well and having fun. Finally, they came in the spring and saw the newborns. They adored the lambs and calves. And, (12)_____! The year was over before I was ready for it to be. It was a great change, and I went back to the city revitalized. I may even return to life on a farm in the near future.

Interactive Exercise | Chapter 12 Review

Answer the following questions to further test your understanding of the vocabulary words.

1. Would you be interested in meeting your doppelgänger? Explain why or why not.

   _____

2. What are two activities where fortitude is essential?

   _____   _____

3. What kind of terrain do you enjoy walking on?

   _____

4. Name two norms for classroom behavior.

   _____   _____

5. What kind of expedition would you like to be invited to join?

   _____

6. What are two pervasive problems in American society?

   _____   _____

7. If decorum were required at a party, describe two ways a person would act.

   _____   _____

8. Name two situations where it would be good to have *nada*.

   _____   _____

9. Give two examples of conventional business attire?

   _____   _____

10. Name two Olympic sports in which the execution of the activity is scored.

    _____   _____

11. What are two actions that a committee might censure one of its members for doing?

    _____   _____

12. How would you describe the zeitgeist at the beginning of a term? Is there a different zeitgeist at the end of the term?

    _____

    _____

HINT

Mistakes as Learning Experiences

Making mistakes is part of the learning process. When you learned to ride a bike, you probably fell over a few times before you learned to keep your balance. The same idea applies to learning vocabulary. When you take a test, you may not get a perfect score. Look at the mistakes you made. Try to decide what went wrong. Did you read the question too fast? Did you misunderstand the question? Did you not study enough? Don't be so disappointed in a bad grade that you can't learn from the experience. You will do better next time if you take the time to understand what you did wrong this time. Also ask your instructor if you are unsure about why you got a question wrong; he or she wants to help you do better next time.

Crossword Puzzle

Use the following words to complete the crossword puzzle. You will use each word once.

VOCABULARY LIST

alfresco

cacophony

clamor

decorum

deviate

doppelgänger

escapade

inception

nada

peninsula

pervasive

plateau

pristine

repertoire

status

stratification

taboo

terrain

voilà

zeitgeist

Across

2. all the works a performer is prepared to present
9. I'm going to take a different road to work today.
12. a start
13. nothing
14. could be high or low in the community
16. a ghostly double
18. a picnic in the park
19. found in royalty and the military

Down

1. the spirit of the time
3. an adventure
4. unspoiled; pure
5. having the quality to spread throughout
6. a harsh, jarring sound
7. has a narrow strip of land connecting it with the mainland
8. forbidden from use or mention
10. heard while building a tree house
11. There it is!
15. could be flat or hilly
16. dignified conduct
17. a stable state

Mix It Up

Matching Meanings

Get four to six classmates together, and make teams of two to three people. You will need two sets of flash cards. Lay out a square of 25 flash cards with the words face up. Lay out another square of the same 25 words with the definitions face up. (You can make larger or smaller squares, but it is best to have at least fifteen words and no more than forty.) One person on a team picks up a word and tries to find the matching definition in the other square. Teammates can help the person. If the person is right, he or she gets to keep both cards. If the person is wrong, he or she returns the cards to their places. A team can keep going until it misses a match. When all the words and definitions are matched, the team with the most cards wins. This activity can also be played with pairs, or you can test yourself individually if you have two sets of flash cards (or you can write the words on slips of paper and match them to the definition side of your flash cards).

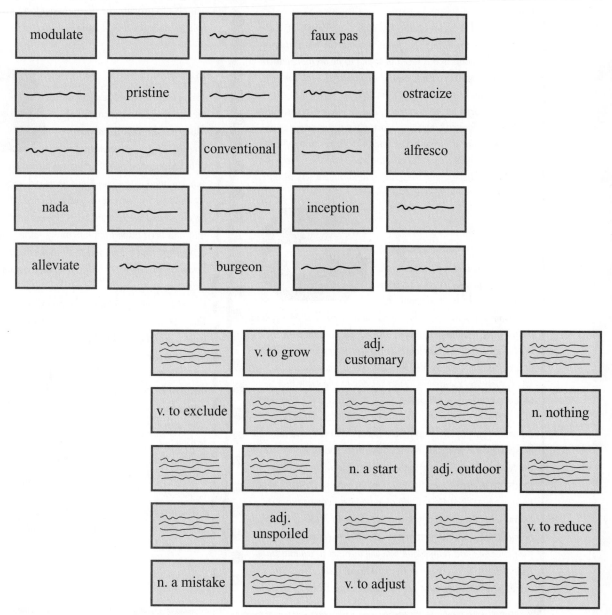

Mongolia Explored

Day 1

On our arrival in Ulaanbaatar, the capital of Mongolia, we were given an orientation. We learned about the **multitude** of problems the country has faced in trying to be an independent nation while dealing with two large neighbors: China and Russia. China ruled Mongolia from 1691 to 1911, when the country declared its independence. Russia offered its assistance to the newly formed country. Unfortunately, the strong communist government of the Soviet Union took over running the country until 1991. Now the country has established itself as a democracy. This is going to be an exciting three weeks as our class explores the history of Mongolia.

Day 2

We are spending the night in gers, the round felt tents of the **nomadic** Mongolian people. A ger (a yurt in Russian) can be built in about an hour, and it is easily portable by camel or oxen. The Mongolian people have traditionally moved around the country with their herds looking for pasture land, so the ger makes for a sensible type of housing. We learned how important animals are to Mongolian life. Goats are important due to their soft hair, known as cashmere, which is made into products like blankets and shirts that are among one of the main items Mongolia **exports**. One popular saying here is that "Mongols are born on horseback." Horse racing is one of the three sports we will see at the Nadam festival, along with wrestling and archery. These sports are referred to as "the three manly games," though women now also participate in the riding and archery competitions. Estimates put the history of the games back to 3000 B.C., when nomadic tribes would meet in the summer to demonstrate their shooting and riding skills. We will also get to try mutton, a Mongolian staple, cooked in the traditional fashion with hot stones in a pot along with water, onions, and spices. Our guide was able to **procure** the sheep from a local family who will show us how to make the dish. I can't wait to taste it.

Day 3

Today we arrived in Karakorum, the site of the ancient capital of Mongolia. We learned about Genghis Khan, the **venerated** ruler of the Mongolian people. After his father was poisoned by rivals, Temujin, who was around nine years old, was left to die in the cold. He survived the winter and vowed revenge. He found allies and began raiding neighboring tribes. He restored the sheep and horses that had been taken from him on his father's death. He continued conquering rival tribes, and at thirty he was the acknowledged leader of the region. In 1206, he took the name Genghis Khan (meaning great king or leader). He was a fierce warrior known for showing no mercy to those who opposed him. After his death in 1227, his son Ogodei used the taxes **levied** on conquered lands to build a grand capital at Karakorum. The **affluence** of the Mongol Empire was evident in the lavish palaces and fountains found in the city. The power of the Mongol Empire began to **wane** after the death of Genghis Khan's grandson Kublai Khan in 1294. The empire had become too big to keep united, and tribes began to fight with each other. In 1368, Chinese rebels burnt Karakorum leaving but a few stones as reminders of the empire's great past. Still **posterity** remembers Genghis Khan as the man who united Mongolia. The Mongol Empire contained the largest area of connected land at any time in history. The territory stretched from Korea to Hungary and into China, Iran, and Iraq. I'm sure that in the **annals** of history, the achievements of Genghis Khan and his descendents will not soon be forgotten.

Predicting

For each set, write the definition on the line next to the word to which it belongs. If you are unsure, return to the reading on page 80, and underline any context clues you find. After you've made your predictions, check your answers against the Word List on page 85. Place a checkmark in the box next to each word whose definition you missed. These are the words you'll want to study closely.

Set One

sends overseas	regarded with respect	the quality of being numerous	wandering	to obtain

☐ 1. **multitude** (line 3) _____

☐ 2. **nomadic** (line 15) _____

☐ 3. **exports** (line 25) _____

☐ 4. **procure** (line 35) _____

☐ 5. **venerated** (line 41) _____

Set Two

to decrease	future generations	imposed	wealth	historical events in general

☐ 6. **levied** (line 51) _____

☐ 7. **affluence** (line 52) _____

☐ 8. **wane** (line 54) _____

☐ 9. **posterity** (line 59) _____

☐ 10. **annals** (line 63) _____

Self-Tests

1 Match each word with its synonym in Set One and its antonym in Set Two.

SYNONYMS

Set One

_____ 1. annals   a. collect

_____ 2. nomadic   b. future

_____ 3. affluence   c. wealth

_____ 4. levy   d. wandering

_____ 5. posterity   e. records

ANTONYMS

Set Two

_____ 6. procure   f. increase

_____ 7. multitude   g. give

_____ 8. venerate   h. degrade

_____ 9. export   i. few

_____ 10. wane   j. import

2 Pick the best word to complete each sentence. Use each word once.

VOCABULARSY LIST

nomadic	waned	multitude	exports	affluence
levy	annals	procure	venerate	posterity

1. My enthusiasm for the project _____ as people began to argue with each other at every meeting.

2. My brother was able to _____ two seats to the sold-out concert for us through his business connections.

3. I had to hand my paper in late because of a(n) _____ of problems, from being sick to computer failures.

4. Among Italy's _____ are wine and olives.

5. We should _____ our nation's teachers because they have much of the responsibility for educating the future.

6. I have been reading the _____ our local historical society has kept about our town. I have discovered some fascinating information about the town's founders and my ancestors.

7. I come from a(n) _____ family. No one in my family stays anywhere for more than a year, whether that means moving to a new city or a new apartment across town.

8. People measure _____ differently. For many people it means money, but for others it means friends, experiences, or even having free time.

9. Next summer, the local recreational area is going to _____ a parking fee on the weekends to help pay for new ball fields and play structures.

10. It would be nice if _____ would remember us as a peace-loving people, but the number of wars in the twentieth century probably makes that hope unrealistic.

3 Answer each question with the appropriate vocabulary word. Use each word once.

VOCABULARY LIST

annals	waned	venerates	levy	nomadic
exports	affluence	procure	posterity	multitude

1. Matt has to feed 300 people. What term would describe this group? _____

2. Alexander needs to get food and drinks for the party. What does he need to do? _____

3. Colleen thinks her grandpa is the smartest man in the world. How does she feel about him? _____

4. The people of the Sahara Desert travel from one watering spot to another. What can their lifestyle be described as? _____

5. Most people today want to keep the air and oceans clean. Who are they saving them for? _____

6. A company based in Spain sends its products to the United States. What does it do with these goods? _____

7. A couple drives a Jaguar, wears designer clothes, and eats at the most expensive restaurants in town. What are they displaying? _____

8. After two years of studying art, it no longer excites Sabrina. What has happened to her interest in the subject? _____

9. The city now charges a fee to use the community pool. What has it started to do? _____

10. The secretary records all of the significant events that happen in the philosophical society during the year and puts them into chronological order. What is she writing? _____

Word Wise

Collocations

The state has decided to *levy a fee* for using all its parks whether people come for an afternoon picnic or to camp overnight. (Chapter 13)

In some cultures grandparents are *highly venerated* for their years of accumulated wisdom. (Chapter 13)

Word Pairs

Export/Import: Export (Chapter 13) means "to send overseas," and import means "to bring in from a foreign country." Among the items Mongolia exports are cashmere, wool, and copper; the country imports fuel, cars, and sugar.

Wax/Wane: Wax means "to increase," and wane (Chapter 13) means "to decrease." The moon waxes each month before the full moon and wanes after it.

Interesting Etymologies

Affluence (Chapter 13): comes from the Latin *ad*, "to," plus *fluere*, "flow" and meant "flowing abundantly." The plentiful flowing eventually came to mean "wealth or abundance."

Interactive Exercise

Finish the following who, what, where, when, and why lists to practice using the vocabulary words. Give two examples for each question.

Genghis Khan

1. Whom do you venerate?

   _____   _____

2. Who will go down in the annals of war as a great leader or warrior?

   _____   _____

3. What would you procure for a picnic?

   _____   _____

4. What items show someone's affluence?

   _____   _____

5. Where would you find a multitude of people?

   _____   _____

6. Where would you like to export goods or ideas to?

   _____   _____

7. Why might a student's attention in class begin to wane?

   _____   _____

8. Why should we care about posterity?

   _____   _____

9. When would a town decide it needs to levy more fees?

   _____   _____

10. When do people tend to be nomadic?

    _____   _____

Word List

affluence
[af′ loo əns]
n. 1. wealth; an abundance
2. a flowing toward

annals
[an′ əlz]
n. yearly historical records, usually in chronological order; historical events in general

export
v. [ek′ spôrt′, -spōrt′, ik spôrt′]
v. 1. to send overseas, especially items for trade or sale
2. to trigger the spread of in a different part of the world; to transmit

n. [eks′ pôrt, -pōrt]
n. an item that is exported

levy
[lev′ ē]
v. to impose or to collect, such as a tax

multitude
[mul′ tə tood′]
n. 1. the quality of being numerous
2. a great, indefinite number
3. the masses

nomadic
[nō′ mad′ ik]
adj. moving from place to palce for surival; wandering; mobile

posterity
[po ster′ ə tē]
n. 1. future generations
2. all of a person's descendants

procure
[prō kyoor′, prə-]
v. to obtain; to get by extra care or effort

venerate
[ven′ ə rāt′]
v. to regard with respect and reverence

wane
[wān]
v. 1. to decrease; to decline
2. to approach an end
n. a gradual declining

Words to Watch

Which words would you like to practice with a bit more? Pick 3–5 words to study, and list them below. Write the word and its definition, and compose your own sentence using the word correctly. This extra practice could be the final touch to learning a word.

	Word	Definition	Your Sentence
1.			
2.			
3.			
4.			
5.			

Speech

Tips for Any Occasion

Speeches come in various forms. You may need to inform, persuade, or entertain your audience. You may have had weeks or months to prepare, or you may have to give an **impromptu** speech with little or no time to gather your thoughts. You
5 could give a speech to ten good friends or before thousands of strangers. You might be asked to speak at a wedding or a board meeting. The following are some tips you can use for any kind of speaking engagement.

   If it is appropriate to your topic and audience, using **levity**
10 to begin a speech can help you and your audience to relax. By telling a joke or an amusing **anecdote**, you may find that you win your audience over in the first few minutes. People enjoy hearing stories, and when the stories are about the speaker, they can be particularly effective.

15   As you plan your speech, make sure your examples are **relevant** to your topic. You should use examples that deal with the subject you are talking about. For example, if your speech is on pollution, you will want to give examples of how bad the water supply is or how poor the air quality has become, not tell how you burned a casserole last night. Also, make sure that you check the
20 **verity** of any statements you make. You want to be accurate in what you say.

   Another way to support your statements is by using expert **testimony**. Find people who are authorities on your topic, and quote them to back up your views. Before you use those people as sources, find out what their credentials are and whether other people in the profession respect them.

   Think about the **ramifications** of your statements. What impact will your comments have on your
25 listeners? Also beware of making **derogatory** statements. You shouldn't belittle your listeners or make negative statements about gender, race, or other characteristics.

   A technique that can make your speech vivid is **visualization**. Use words that will help listeners see what you are talking about. Describe the people and places that are important to your speech by using sensory details. Tell how something sounded, smelled, or tasted.

30   Lastly, don't forget a **summation** that covers your main points. Remember that your closing is your last chance to reach your audience. If there is something you want them to remember, tell them once again. Give your speech a sense of conclusion. Don't leave your audience feeling that something is missing.

   Using these simple techniques can help you feel more confident any time you are asked to step up
35 to the podium.

Predicting

For each set, write the definition on the line next to the word to which it belongs. If you are unsure, return to the reading on page 86, and underline any context clues you find. After you've made your predictions, check your answers against the Word List on page 91. Place a checkmark in the box next to each word whose definition you missed. These are the words you'll want to study closely.

Set One

to the point	a short account	spontaneous
the quality of being real or correct	lightness of speech or manner	

❏ 1. **impromptu** (line 3) _____

❏ 2. **levity** (line 9) _____

❏ 3. **anecdote** (line 11) _____

❏ 4. **relevant** (line 16) _____

❏ 5. **verity** (line 20) _____

Set Two

proof	insulting	a concluding statement
developments	the formation of a mental image	

❏ 6. **testimony** (line 21) _____

❏ 7. **ramifications** (line 24) _____

❏ 8. **derogatory** (line 25) _____

❏ 9. **visualization** (line 27) _____

❏ 10. **summation** (line 30) _____

Self-Tests

1 Match each word with its synonym in Set One and its antonym in Set Two.

SYNONYMS

Set One

_____ 1. summation   a. image

_____ 2. testimony   b. result

_____ 3. visualization   c. addition

_____ 4. ramification   d. story

_____ 5. anecdote   e. proof

ANTONYMS

Set Two

_____	6. verity	f. supportive
_____	7. levity	g. unrelated
_____	8. relevant	h. seriousness
_____	9. derogatory	i. planned
_____	10. impromptu	j. untrue

2 Finish the sentences. Use each word once.

VOCABULARY LIST

levity	testimony	anecdote	visualization	summation
derogatory	verity	impromptu	relevant	ramification

1. When I want to relax, I use _____ to picture myself sleeping in a meadow filled with flowers.

2. My sister told me a funny _____ about trying to get her son to bed.

3. I have to give a(n) _____ speech tomorrow; I hope my instructor gives me a subject I know at least a little about.

4. We needed some _____ in the room after Steve spent half an hour telling us about his gallbladder operation.

5. I got up and left the meeting when the speaker started to make _____ statements about my college.

6. I wanted to believe the man's _____, but the way he kept looking down made me think he was lying.

7. The _____ of arriving twenty minutes late didn't occur to me until I looked at the timetable and saw that we would just miss the ferry.

8. I wasn't sure about the _____ of the speaker's assertion that the moon is one hundred miles from the Earth.

9. I need to find a book on snakes because I think it will have _____ examples for my talk on dangerous animals.

10. In her _____, the mayor reviewed the major plans for the next year of her term.

3 Use the vocabulary words to complete the following analogies. For instructions and practice, see Completing Analogies on page 4.

> **VOCABULARY LIST**
>
> | levity | testimony | anecdote | visualization | summation |
> |---|---|---|---|---|
> | derogatory | verity | impromptu | relevant | ramification |

1. shopper : customer :: story : _____
2. complimentary : you have a beautiful home :: _____ : what an ugly house
3. bought a new sweater : purchase :: the sun is hot : _____
4. insult : anger :: joke : _____
5. escape : disappearance :: branching out : _____
6. exercise : take a long walk :: _____ : picture a sunny beach
7. unconnected : unrelated :: pertinent : _____
8. charity : I gave fifty dollars to the Cancer Society :: _____ : I saw him rob the bank
9. intended : planned :: _____ : spontaneous
10. first : last :: opening : _____

Word Wise

Context Clue Mini-Lesson 4

This lesson uses the general meaning of a sentence or passage to help you understand the meaning of the underlined word. In the paragraph below, circle any words that give you clues to the meaning. Write your definitions of the underlined words in the blanks that follow the paragraph.

The area looked <u>devoid</u> of any chance for life. The ground was hard, and the few plants around looked dead. But the pioneers felt the land was <u>arable</u>. They carefully tended the land, and within five years it was transformed into a <u>verdant</u> paradise. Orchards of apples and pears sprinkled the landscape; lettuce, corn, and other vegetables filled the fields; and flowering trees adorned each yard. The pioneers had known that to <u>cultivate</u> the area all they needed was patience and hard work, which they had gladly supplied.

Your Definition

1. Devoid _____
2. Arable _____
3. Verdant _____
4. Cultivate _____

Pretend that you are preparing a speech on why the cafeteria needs better food. Make your answers to all but Question 10 deal with this topic.

1. Write an anecdote you could begin your speech with.

   _____

   _____

2. Give two examples that would be relevant to this topic.

   _____   _____

3. Who could give expert testimony on food?

   _____

4. Explain one way you could check on the verity of the manager's statement: "Providing healthy food is just too expensive for the cafeteria."

   _____

5. In using visualization, to which two senses would you want to appeal the most?

   _____   _____

6. How could you add levity to your talk?

   _____

7. What might be one ramification of your speech?

   _____

8. What type of derogatory statement should you avoid using?

   _____

9. Write a sentence that would be part of your summation.

   _____

10. If you had to give an impromptu talk about something, on what topic would you speak?

    _____

HINT

Meeting with a Study Group

To create an effective study session, keep these points in mind.

- Pick a place to meet that is beneficial for studying. Find a place where it's easy to talk, but where you won't be interrupted by distractions. Check on the availability of group study rooms in the library.
- Bring the necessary books, notes, and other materials to each session.
- Ask various group members to be "the expert" on different chapters or areas of study—have them share their in-depth study with the other group members. Give everyone a chance to participate, and respect each person's views.
- Assign someone to keep the group on track and be aware of time limits. Gently remind people who start to talk about other topics that you are all there to study. Ask anyone to leave who does not really want to study.
- Evaluate how useful the study session was, and decide what changes may be needed for the next time. Try to make the study sessions fun and productive.

Word List

anecdote
[an′ ik dōt′]
n. a short account of an interesting or amusing incident

derogatory
[di rog′ ə tôr′ ē]
adj. offensive; insulting; critical

impromptu
[im promp′ tōō]
adj. not rehearsed; spontaneous

levity
[lev′ ə tē]
n. 1. lightness of speech or manner; frivolity
2. lightness; buoyancy

ramification
[ram′ ə fi kā′ shən]
n. 1. a development growing out of and often complicating a problem, plan, or statement; a consequence
2. the act of branching out

relevant
[rel′ ə vənt]
adj. pertinent; to the point

summation
[sə mā′ shən]
n. 1. a concluding statement containing a summary of principal points
2. the act of totaling; addition

testimony
[tes′ tə mō′ nē]
n. evidence in support of a fact or assertion; proof

verity
[ver′ ə tē]
n. 1. the quality of being real, accurate, or correct
2. a statement of principle considered to be permanent truth

visualization
[vizh′ ōō ə li zā′ shən]
n. the formation of a mental image or images

Words to Watch

Which words would you like to practice with a bit more? Pick 3–5 words to study, and list them below. Write the word and its definition, and compose your own sentence using the word correctly. This extra practice could be the final touch to learning a word.

	Word	Definition	Your Sentence
1.			
2.			
3.			
4.			
5.			

Well Worth Watching

Classic Movie Corner

If you are looking for a great movie to spend time with this weekend, here are two classics that won't disappoint you, even if you have seen them before.

Psycho (1960)

5 *Wild Strawberries* (1957)

Ingmar Bergman's *Wild Strawberries* has
10 been **hailed** as a masterpiece, and it is a film that deserves its reputation. Bergman wrote
15 and directed the film. The movie takes viewers into the mind of Isak Borg, an elderly gentleman, as he embarks on a long car trip to receive an honorary degree. The **cinematography** brilliantly uses black-and-white contrasts to show his
20 disturbed thoughts. **Surreal** dream sequences take us into his past and into his **disconcerted** mind. Clocks without hands and an examination room with strange questions are among the unusual experiences Dr. Borg faces. The
25 **juxtapositions** of old age and youth (both Borg's youth and the young people he meets on his journey) force us, as well as the doctor, to examine life and our actions. As this is a film you will want to discuss after viewing, invite your
30 friends over to share ideas on what the dream sequences might mean and what Bergman may have wanted people to gain from seeing the movie.

The film stars Victor Sjostrom, Bibi Andersson,
35 Ingrid Thulin, Gunnar Bjornstand, and Max Von Sydow. Swedish. 90 minutes.

Alfred Hitchcock's films are a must for the **connoisseur** of the suspense **genre**, and *Psycho* is one of his best films. Whether you have seen it 40 once, twice, or a hundred times, it is worth another viewing, and if you have never seen it, it is about time you did. Hitchcock was marvelously **attuned** to the darker sides of human nature, and he was able to convey the fears and desires of lust 45 and greed in fascinating images. In the famous shower scene, for example, Hitchcock uses **montage** to create the suspense. Through careful editing, he creates tension in the audience while barely showing the plunging knife touch the 50 victim. In fact, Hitchcock put seventy-eight short shots together to create the scene. For many people, *Psycho* **epitomizes** the suspense movie. It holds all the thrills an audience expects from the unexpected. Hitchcock masterfully used lighting, 55 camera movements, and music to create the terror one craves in a suspense movie, unlike many of the disappointing horror films of today that reveal too much, too fast, and too predictably. Norman Bates continues to reign as one of the scariest 60 characters in film history.

The film stars Anthony Perkins, Vera Miles, John Gavin, Martin Balsam, John McIntire, and Janet Leigh. American. 108 minutes.

Predicting ||||||||||||||||||||||||||||||||||||||||||||||||||||||||||||||||||||||

For each set, write the definition on the line next to the word to which it belongs. If you are unsure, return to the reading on page 92, and underline any context clues you find. After you've made your predictions, check your answers against the Word List on page 97. Place a checkmark in the box next to each word whose definition you missed. These are the words you'll want to study closely.

Set One

fantastic	approved enthusiastically	disturbed
the art of motion picture photography	acts of placing close together	

☐ 1. **hailed** (line 9) _____

☐ 2. **cinematography** (line 18) _____

☐ 3. **surreal** (line 20) _____

☐ 4. **disconcerted** (line 21) _____

☐ 5. **juxtapositions** (line 25) _____

Set Two

a style	a film editing technique	a person who can judge the best in a field
serves as a typical or perfect example of	adjusted	

☐ 6. **connoisseur** (line 39) _____

☐ 7. **genre** (line 39) _____

☐ 8. **attuned** (line 44) _____

☐ 9. **montage** (line 48) _____

☐ 10. **epitomizes** (line 53) _____

Self-Tests ||||||||||||||||||||||||||||||||||||||||||||||||||||||||||||||||||||||

1 Circle the correct meaning of each vocabulary word.

1. hail:	welcome	ignore
2. connoisseur:	unsure of quality	judge of the best
3. genre:	a style	an exception
4. montage:	separate	combining to form a whole
5. attune:	adjust	clash
6. epitomize:	typify	conceal
7. disconcerted:	clear	confused
8. surreal:	fantastic	factual
9. cinematography:	art of writing	art of motion picture photography
10. juxtaposition:	putting far apart	placing close together

2 These comments are overheard as people file out of the multiplex movie theater. Match each sentence to the word it best fits. Use each word once.

VOCABULARY LIST

genre	surreal	attuned	disconcerted	juxtaposition
montage	hail	epitomize	connoisseur	cinematography

1. "The desert scenes were beautifully filmed. They really showed the richness of color in the sand and the sunsets." _____

2. "That was a great film! It's going to be the year's best movie!" _____

3. "Even though it was so strange, I liked it when everyone started flying around and speaking that strange language." _____

4. "I had to get used to the relaxed pace of the movie, but once I did, I really enjoyed the film." _____

5. "I am an expert on horror movies, and I can tell you this was not one of the director's best efforts." _____

6. "It really disturbed me when the movie began jumping back and forth between the past and the present." _____

7. "Next time we are staying home and renting Westerns; those are my kinds of movies." _____

8. "It was interesting how the blonde woman was standing next to old cars in so many scenes. I think the director was trying to make a point about stereotypes in America." _____

9. "That film is a perfect example of everything I dislike about musicals, especially having people break into a song every ten minutes." _____

10. "I liked the part where the director put the various shots of prison life together to show the boredom of the prisoners." _____

3 Finish the sentences. Use each word once.

VOCABULARY LIST

epitomized	attuned	connoisseur	surreal	juxtaposition
montage	hailed	disconcerted	genre	cinematography

1. My father is a chocolate _____; he will eat nothing but the finest European chocolates.

2. The newspaper reviewer loved the concert; she _____ it as the best performance in the symphony's twenty-year history.

3. The _____ of scenes on a quiet beach with the freeway traffic really showed that the character needed to escape the pressures of the big city.

4. The vivid colors used in the film caused me to pay attention to the _____ over the other elements such as music and plot.

5. By being _____ to the latest trends, some producers can create a movie that capitalizes on a fad such as skateboarding or disco dancing.

6. It is easy to become _____ in today's multi-plex theaters; I went to get popcorn and couldn't find my way back without asking an usher for directions.

7. On movie night we make a bowl of popcorn, and we each select a film from our favorite _____ to watch. I pick a musical, and my husband chooses an action film.

8. In *Battleship Potemkin*, Eisenstein's skillful editing of scenes showing the poor treatment of the sailors creates a powerful _____ that depicts the men's discontent.

9. The scene where the man threw the puppy off the roof _____ his evil nature.

10. It was a(n) _____ experience when I woke up in a hotel room and thought I was in my own bedroom.

Word Wise

A Different Approach: Word Groups

Putting words into related groups can be a way to help your mind organize new vocabulary. To create word groups, get a piece of paper, pick a category, and list as many of the vocabulary words whose definitions fit under that heading in a general way. You will, of course, need to know the shades of meaning the more frequently you use a word. The academic subjects used in each chapter of this book are already one way to organize some of the words. You will want to come up with other categories as you study words from multiple chapters. For example, here are four words to begin a sample list of eight vocabulary words that fit the category of "the arts": vivid (Chapter 2), repertoire and execution (Chapter 8), and cinematography (Chapter 15). As you work through the book, look for four other words that would fit this category, and return here to complete the list.

1. _____
2. _____
3. _____
4. _____

Other possible categories are "science words," "business words," "qualities a person would want to have," and "undesirable characteristics." For a fun and collaborative way to use word groups, see the directions for Category Race in Chapter 18.

Interactive Exercise

Answer the following questions.

1. What is your favorite movie genre? _____

2. What might happen in a surreal dream?_____

   _____

3. What would look unusual juxtaposed next to a piece of fruit?_____

   _____

4. What are you a connoisseur of, or what would you like to be a connoisseur of?_____

   _____

5. What can you do to be better attuned to the feelings of others? _____

   _____

   _____

6. Which movie star do you think epitomizes style?_____

7. What movie do you think has beautiful cinematography?_____

   _____

8. What could happen in a movie to make you feel disconcerted?_____

   _____

   _____

9. What would you hail as a great achievement of humankind?_____

   _____

   _____

10. If you were to create a montage showing the first day of kindergarten, what are three images you would use?_____

    _____

    _____

Word Part Reminder

Below are a few short exercises to help you review the word parts you have been learning. Fill in the missing word part from the list, and circle the meaning of the word part found in each sentence. Try to complete the questions without returning to the Word Parts chapters, but if you get stuck, look back at Chapter 11.

phobia	ex	flux	port

1. I want to buy a fan that is easy to carry, so I will look for a _____able model.

2. I have a fear of fire; my pyro_____ has prevented me from ever roasting marshmallows at our annual campout.

3. When I was a kid, the boys tried to keep us out of their clubhouse, but we didn't let them _____clude us on days when they had cookies.

4. New students have been flowing into the college this semester. I don't know what has led to this sudden in_____.

Word List

attune
[ə to͞on′, ə tyo͞on′]

v. to adjust; to bring into harmony

cinematography
[sin′ ə mə tog′ rə fē]

n. the art or technique of motion picture photography

connoisseur
[kon′ ə sûr′, -soor′]

n. a person who can judge the best in an art or other field

disconcerted
[dis′ kən sûrt′ əd]

adj. disturbed; disordered; confused

epitomize
[i pit′ ə mīz′]

v. to serve as a typical or perfect example of; to typify

genre
[zhän′ rə]

n. a class of artistic work (movie, book, etc.) having a particular form, content, or technique; a style

hail
[hāl]

v. 1. to approve enthusiastically
2. to cheer; to welcome; to call out to

juxtaposition
[juk′ stə pə zish′ ən]

n. an act of placing close together, especially for comparison or contrast

montage
[mon täzh′]

n. 1. a film editing technique that presents images next to each other to convey an action, idea, or feeling
2. the combining of various elements to form a whole or single image

surreal
[sə rē′ əl, -rēl′]

adj. unreal; fantastic; having the quality of a dream

Words to Watch

Which words would you like to practice with a bit more? Pick 3–5 words to study, and list them below. Write the word and its definition, and compose your own sentence using the word correctly. This extra practice could be the final touch to learning a word.

Word	Definition	Your Sentence
1. _____	_____	_____
2. _____	_____	_____
3. _____	_____	_____
4. _____	_____	_____
5. _____	_____	_____

Anthropology

Societies and Customs

The Mayan culture continues to intrigue modern
society. One of the great centers of Mayan culture was
Chichen-Itza on the Yucatan Peninsula. Life at
Chichen-Itza was hardly **immutable**. Roughly between
5 500 and 1400, a site of numerous temples, a huge ball
court, and an astronomical observatory burgeoned in
the tropical jungle. The Maya abandoned the site twice,
and around 1200 the Toltecs from the north invaded the
area, adding their religion and architecture to the
10 Mayan concepts. Anthropologists and archeologists
have been **meticulous** in studying the ruins at Chichen-
Itza to discover the customs of this ancient society.

What made life **viable** for the Maya at Chichen-
Itza were the *cenotes*, or wells. The name *chichen*
15 shows the importance of the wells to the society. *Chi*
meant "mouths" in Mayan, and *chen* meant "wells."
These wells provided a source of water for a community composed of a **hierarchy** of slaves, farmers,
hunters, merchants, warriors, priests, and nobles. Each group had its special role to play to keep the
20 community functioning. The cenotes also hold a clue to the religious **rituals** of the Maya: several
bodies have been found in the wells. Human sacrifice, though generally considered **heinous** by today's
standards, was a part of Mayan religious practices. Other **artifacts** found in the cenotes include jewelry
and dolls. The Maya had several gods, and the sacrifices of young women and objects may have been
used to **quell** the wrath of a rain god or pay homage to the god of maize. Because the gods controlled
25 the weather and therefore the food supply, it was essential for the people to keep the gods happy.
Bloodletting, especially of the ears and tongue, was another way a person could earn favor with a god.

Religious beliefs were also **manifested** in the architecture and games of the Maya. An impressive
and **ominous** area at Chichen-Itza is the Great Ball Court, the largest found at a Mayan site. The ball-
game was played between two teams and seems to have involved
30 keeping a rubber ball from touching the ground without using the
hands. The game was over when the ball went through a scoring
ring attached to the walls of the court. The winner of the game did
not receive the prize people today would expect. The captain of
the winning team would offer his head to the leader of the losing
35 team for decapitation. It was part of the Mayan religious beliefs
that dying quickly was a great honor, and they obviously felt that
the winner of this contest deserved such an honor.

The Maya were a highly advanced society, demonstrated in
their complex temple designs, accurate calendar, and elaborate
40 artwork. The Maya continue to fascinate the world with their
customs and achievements.

The Castillo

*A chacmool figure introduced by the
Toltecs, possibly used in heart sacrifices*

Predicting ||||||||||||||||||||||||||||||||||||||||||||||||||||||||||||||||||||||||||||||||||||||||||||||||

For each set, write the definition on the line next to the word to which it belongs. If you are unsure, return to the reading on page 98, and underline any context clues you find. After you've made your predictions, check your answers against the Word List on page 103. Place a checkmark in the box next to each word whose definition you missed. These are the words you'll want to study closely.

Set One

> possible   set procedures for a ceremony   unchangeable
>
> extremely careful   a system of persons ranked one above the other

☐ 1. **immutable** (line 4) _____

☐ 2. **meticulous** (line 11) _____

☐ 3. **viable** (line 13) _____

☐ 4. **hierarchy** (line 18) _____

☐ 5. **rituals** (line 20) _____

Set Two

> any objects made by humans   revealed   evil   to quiet   threatening

☐ 6. **heinous** (line 21) _____

☐ 7. **artifacts** (line 22) _____

☐ 8. **quell** (line 24) _____

☐ 9. **manifested** (line 27) _____

☐ 10. **ominous** (line 28) _____

Self-Tests ||||||||||||||||||||||||||||||||||||||||||||||||||||||||||||||||||||||||||||||||||||||||||||||

1 Match each term with its synonym in Set One and its antonym in Set Two.

SYNONYMS
Set One

_____ 1. heinous   a. workable

_____ 2. quell   b. object

_____ 3. meticulous   c. calm

_____ 4. artifact   d. vicious

_____ 5. viable   e. thorough

ANTONYMS
Set Two

_____ 6. ritual   f. equality

_____ 7. immutable   g. hidden

_____ 8. hierarchy   h. variety

_____ 9. ominous   i. changeable

_____ 10. manifest   j. safe

2 Complete the sentences using the vocabulary words. Use each word once.

1. My mother's negative reaction was _____; she would never approve of my little sister taking a trip to India with a man she met a month ago.

2. The museum displayed _____ from the Inca civilization including beautifully decorated pots.

3. Alicia was quick to _____ the rumor that she was engaged to Brian; she assured people they were just friends.

4. The _____ music signaled the entrance of the villain.

5. The people decided that the mountain was not a(n) _____ place to live after their crops failed two years in a row.

6. His love for Amanda was _____ to everyone but Carlos.

7. It was a(n) _____ action by the vandals to break all the windows in the auditorium the day before the graduation ceremony.

8. I was _____ in following the instructions for the cake, so I don't understand why it tasted horrible.

9. To get things done at my office, it is essential to understand the _____ from supervisor on down.

10. The _____ practices of different societies are interesting to study, especially marriage customs.

3 Complete the readings using each word once.

DAY 1

The plane is about to take off. I am so excited about my summer trip to the South Pacific to gather information on how the local people live. I am especially excited about seeing their (1)_____.

I became intrigued about island customs after reading Margaret Mead's book *The Coming of Age in Samoa*. Her (2)_____ work in observing and recording the behaviors of the people fascinated me. I am also curious whether the (3)_____ system is still functioning the same or whether people can move between ranks more easily now. I wasn't sure that making a living as an anthropologist was a(n) (4)_____ idea, but when I started college two years ago, I decided to pursue a subject I love. I know that the society I am about to visit has not been (5)_____, but I hope to see some of the practices that my hero Mead saw.

VOCABULARY LIST

heinous	ominous	artifacts	quell	manifest

Today we visited some (6)_____: an army of ancient carved figures used to guard a sacred ceremonial site. The faces were (7)_____ with big eyes and long tongues sticking out of huge mouths. If someone dared to walk past the statues, he or she was sure to anger the gods. The natives believed that (8)_____ troubles would befall a person who entered the taboo area. Because of the strong belief in a statue's power, illnesses could (9)_____ themselves in a person. It took herbal medicines and potent ceremonies to (10)_____ the fears and difficulties of those who disturbed the sacred place.

Word Wise

Collocations

I couldn't stop myself from making a *derogatory remark* about Miranda's favorite football team once she had insulted my favorite team. (Chapter 14)

The outcome of the trial meant the success or failure of the company, so it was filled with *expert testimony* from people involved in all aspects of the business. (Chapter 14)

I was *disconcerted by* Alfred's suggestion that I wasn't telling the whole truth about what I had done over the weekend. (Chapter 15)

Manifest Destiny was the belief that it was inescapable for the United States to expand westward during the 1800s. (Chapter 16)

At work, it can be important to *quell a rumor* before too many people get a wrong idea. (Chapter 16)

Word Pairs

Impromptu/Prepared: Impromptu (Chapter 14) means "not rehearsed; spontaneous." Prepared means "arranged; planned." I was forced to give an impromptu speech on "The Importance of Saving Money" for my speech class. I do much better on the prepared speeches when I have time to research and practice what I want to say.

Interesting Etymologies

Hail (Chapter 15): comes from the Middle English phrase *waes haeil,* "be healthy." The word *wassail,* a drink, also comes from this origin, and it is often drunk during times of well wishing in the December holidays. When a movie is hailed as great, there are well wishes there too. Hail means "to welcome; to call out to" and "to approve enthusiastically."

Interactive Exercise |||||||||||||||||||||||||||||||||||||||||||||||||||||||||||||||||||||||||||||

Give two examples for each question.

1. Where might someone find an artifact?

   _____   _____

2. What should you be meticulous about?

   _____   _____

3. What would most people consider a heinous action?

   _____   _____

4. What would you consider an ominous sign?

   _____   _____

5. How might someone quell the anger of a child?

   _____   _____

6. Where might you find a hierarchy?

   _____   _____

7. What things are immutable?

   _____   _____

8. What rituals does your family have?

   _____   _____

9. How might someone manifest his or her love for a person?

   _____   _____

10. What would be a viable vacation plan for you this year?

   _____   _____

Conversation Starters

An excellent way to review the vocabulary words and help to make them your own is to use them when you are speaking. Gather three to five friends or classmates, and use one or more of the conversation starters below. Before you begin talking, have each person write down six of the vocabulary words he or she will use during the conversation. Share your lists with each other to check that you did not pick the same six words. Try to cover all of the words you want to study, whether you are reviewing one, two, or more chapters.

1. What are two events that you think have been significant in world history? Why are these events important? Who do you think has been one of the greatest rulers in world history?

2. How do you feel about giving speeches? Do you get nervous? Would you rather give a speech before a group of strangers or your family and friends? What has influenced your decision between the two?

3. What are two movies you have enjoyed watching? What did you like about them? What is a movie you didn't like? What caused you to dislike it?

4. What culture would you be interested in studying? What attracts you to this culture? Are you more interested in past cultures that no longer exist or isolated but surviving groups?

Word List

artifact
[är′ tə fakt′]

n. any object made by humans; a handmade object or the remains of one, such as found at an archeological dig

heinous
[hā′ nəs]

adj. wicked; vile; evil

hierarchy
[hī′ ə rär′ kē, hī′ rär′ kē]

n. a system of persons or things ranked one above the other

immutable
[i myoo′ tə bəl]

adj. unchangeable

manifest
[man′ ə fest′]

v. to reveal; to show plainly
adj. obvious; evident

meticulous
[mə tik′ yə ləs]

adj. 1. extremely careful and precise
2. excessively concerned with details

ominous
[om′ ə nəs]

adj. 1. threatening; menacing
2. pertaining to an evil omen

quell
[kwel]

v. 1. to quiet; to pacify
2. to suppress

ritual
[rich′ oo əl]

n. 1. a set procedure for a religious or other ceremony
2. a custom; a routine
adj. 1. ceremonial
2. customary; routine

viable
[vī′ ə bəl]

adj. 1. practicable; possible
2. capable of living or developing

Words to Watch

Which words would you like to practice with a bit more? Pick 3–5 words to study, and list them below. Write the word and its definition, and compose your own sentence using the word correctly. This extra practice could be the final touch to learning a word.

	Word	Definition	Your Sentence
1.	_____	_____	_____
	_____		
2.	_____	_____	_____
	_____		
3.	_____	_____	_____
	_____		
4.	_____	_____	_____
	_____		
5.	_____	_____	_____
	_____		

Look for words with these **prefixes, roots,** and/or **suffixes** as you work through this book. You may have already seen some of them, and you will see others in later chapters. Learning basic word parts can help you figure out the meanings of unfamiliar words.

prefix: a word part added to the beginning of a word that changes the meaning of the root
root: a word's basic part with its essential meaning
suffix: a word part added to the end of a word; indicates the part of speech

Word Part	Meaning	Examples and Definitions
Prefixes		
meta-	change	*metamorphosis:* a change in form *metabolism:* chemical changes in an organism
multi-	many, much	*multitude:* an indefinite number; many *multicolored:* many-colored
para-	next to, almost, beyond, abnormal	*paraphrase:* to restate almost like the original *parallel:* next to each other without ever meeting
Roots		
-annu-, -enni-	year	*biannual:* happening twice each year *perennial:* lasting through many years
-mut-	change	*permutation:* the act of changing *mutant:* a new type of organism due to a change
-sequ-	to follow	*inconsequential:* not worth following; unimportant *sequel:* anything that follows; a continuation
-tract-	to drag, to pull, to draw	*abstract:* to draw or pull out *tractor:* a vehicle used to pull things
-trib-	give	*tribute:* something given or done to show respect *contribute:* to give along with others
Suffixes		
-oid (makes an adjective)	like, resembling	*paranoid:* resembling paranoia (a suspicion of others) *humanoid:* resembling humans
-ure (makes a verb)	action or process	*censure:* process of expressing disapproval *failure:* action of failing

Self-Tests

1 Read each definition, and choose the appropriate word. Use each word once. The meaning of the word part is underlined to help you make the connection. Refer to the Word Parts list if you need help.

1. star<u>like</u> _____

2. the <u>process</u> of making something safe _____

3. lasting 100 <u>years</u> _____

4. to <u>give</u> out _____

5. a person trained to work <u>next to</u> a lawyer or teacher _____

6. to draw or <u>pull</u> out _____

7. the <u>change</u> in location of a disease in the body _____

8. having <u>many</u> skills _____

9. to <u>change</u> a penalty to a less severe form _____

10. the <u>following</u> of one thing after another _____

VOCABULARY LIST

asteroid	commute
secure	sequence
distribute	centennial
multitalented	abstract
paraprofessional	metastasis

2 Finish the sentences with the meaning of each word part. Use each meaning once. The word part is underlined to help you make the connection.

VOCABULARY LIST

draw	many	give	process	almost
year	resemble	change	follow	changes

1. Androids are popular characters in science fiction movies because they _____ human beings; therefore, they are easy to costume.

2. The <u>mut</u>ant ant was able to carry twice as much as a normal ant. The _____ made it a valuable addition to the colony.

3. I attribute much of my success as a musician to my fifth-grade music teacher; I _____ him credit for teaching me about the discipline of practicing and the beauty of creating new sounds.

4. The <u>sequel</u> continues to _____ Nita's adventures, but now she is three years older and entering college.

5. My <u>para</u>phrase was _____ like the original quote, but I made sure to use enough of my own words and style to avoid plagiarizing.

6. I was able to <u>pro</u>cure the special chocolates my husband likes, but the _____ wasn't easy. I had to call ten places to find where I could order them.

7. I like the way the writer uses a <u>meta</u>phor to compare the woman's face to a banana. The way he _____ the usual use of the word *banana* clearly shows that the woman has a long, thin face.

8. My husband usually forgets our <u>anni</u>versary, but he remembered this _____.

9. The store was able to _____ me in with their <u>attra</u>ctive window display.

10. Because I work for a <u>multi</u>national corporation, I could be transferred to _____ countries.

3 Finish the story using the word parts. Use each word part once. Your knowledge of word parts, as well as the context clues, will help you create the correct words. If you do not understand the meaning of a word you have made, check the dictionary for the definition or to see whether the word exists.

WORD PARTS LIST

multi	sequ	trib	oid	annu
meta	para	mut	tract	ure

The Baking Battle

It was time for the town's (1)_____al cooking contests, and this year I was going to participate for the third time. This year I was going to con(2)_____ute my extraordinary brownies. I was paran(3)_____ that someone would discover my secret ingredients, so when I went shopping for them, I bought fifty other items. No one who saw me at the store would be able to figure out which ingredients were going into the brownies. My brownies had gone through several per(4)_____ations over the years, but I now felt they were perfect. I carefully followed the proced(5)_____ I had established for making the ultimate brownie. The whole process had to be just right. Finally, the brownies were ready for their (6)_____morphosis. Into the oven they went to change from sticky batter to delicious delights.

In the afternoon, I took my brownies to the judging area. There I met my other competitors. I was upset to see June Elaine with a pan of brownies. She had won so many times in (7)_____ple categories, including cakes, casseroles, and wheat breads. She even won the chili cook-off one year. The judges tasted all fifteen entries twice. Then they adjourned to another room to discuss their choices. They still hadn't emerged after thirty minutes. I thought they were trying to pro(8)_____ the suspense, but I didn't need them to draw it out any longer. I was so nervous. They finally came out and said, "We have an unusual situation this year. We have been unable to decide between two of the entries. Con(9)_____ently, we are going to break with tradition and give two first place awards." I held my breath. I was one of the winners! The other, of course, was June Elaine. I didn't care that we both won first place. I was actually proud to have my brownies in the same league as hers. I even hoped that my entries from now on would (10)_____llel her success.

4 Pick the best definition for each underlined word using your knowledge of word parts. Circle the word part in each of the underlined words.

a. the process of expressing disapproval

b. resembling the truth but unproven

c. a quality given to a person or thing

d. unchangeable

e. a person who changes a literary work from one form to another

f. beyond the usual

g. a comment that doesn't follow the preceding one

h. to draw away

i. happening every two years

j. a university with many campuses

_____ 1. The Internet has helped to spread several <u>factoids</u>; people read the same stories about killer bananas or ways to earn thousands of dollars and think the stories are real.

_____ 2. Tina is studying <u>paranormal</u> activities such as clairvoyance and extrasensory perception.

_____ 3. Going to a <u>multiversity</u> can be tiring. I have to drive to four different campuses this semester to get to all my classes.

_____ 4. The board had to <u>censure</u> the secretary for putting inappropriate remarks in the minutes of the monthly meetings.

_____ 5. An <u>attribute</u> that immediately comes to mind when I think of Elizabeth is friendliness.

_____ 6. Unfortunately, Verda was <u>immutable</u> about her vacation plans, and she went to the mountains to ski even though there wasn't any snow.

_____ 7. I found it hard to understand the speaker because his speech was filled with <u>non sequiturs</u>. His comments just didn't connect to one another.

_____ 8. The Olympics are a <u>biennial</u> celebration of athletics worldwide.

_____ 9. I put the rusted statue in the garage; now it won't <u>detract</u> from the appeal of the house.

_____ 10. My uncle is a <u>metaphrast</u>; he changes short stories into poems.

5 A good way to remember word parts is to pick one word that uses a word part and understand how that word part functions in the word. Then you can apply that meaning to other words that have the same word part. Use the words to help you match the word part to its meaning.

Set One

_____ 1. **multi-:** multitude, multiply, multifaceted

_____ 2. **meta-:** metamorphosis, metaphor, metabolism

_____ 3. **-tract-:** abstract, tractor, attractive

_____ 4. **-sequ-:** sequential, sequel, consequence

_____ 5. **-oid:** humanoid, paranoid, android

a. to follow

b. change

c. many, much

d. to drag, to pull, to draw

e. like, resembling

Set Two

_____ 6. **para-:** parallel, parasite, paranormal

_____ 7. **-trib-:** tribute, contribute, attribute

_____ 8. **-mut-:** permutation, commute, mutation

_____ 9. **-annu-, -enni-:** annual, anniversary, perennial

_____ 10. **-ure:** censure, failure, procedure

f. give

g. year

h. action or process

i. change

j. next to, almost, beyond, abnormal

Interactive Exercise ||||||||||||||||||||||||||||||||||||||||||||||||||||||||||||||||||||||||||||||||||

Use the dictionary to find a word you don't know that uses each word part listed below. Write the meaning of the word part, the word, and the definition. If your dictionary has the etymology (history) of the word, see how the word part relates to the meaning, and write the etymology after the definition.

Word Part	Meaning	Word	Definition and Etymology
EXAMPLE:			
-sequ-	to follow	sequela	an abnormal condition resulting from a previous disease. From Latin "sequela," what follows
1. -annu-			
2. meta-			
3. multi-			
4. -mut-			
5. -tract-			

Word Wise

Internet Activity: For Further Reading and Research

When the readings in this text capture your attention, turn to the Internet for more information. When you see a vocabulary word you have been studying on a Web site, note how it is used. You will also likely come across new words where you can practice your context-clue skills to discover a meaning. Here are a few sites to get you started in your quest for further information.

For more on immigration, Genghis Khan, the Mayans, Julius Caesar, Karl Marx, or the former Soviet Union, try www.historychannel.com. At the History Channel's Web site, type in the time period, person, or event that interests you, and you will find a wide choice of articles to click on.

For science information, visit *National Geographic* magazine at www.nationalgeographic.com or the Discovery Channel site at www.discovery.com. For technology information, try the site for *Wired* magazine: www.wired.com.

To explore the art and entertainment worlds, try www.salon.com for articles on a variety of creative interests from movies to music.

For a list of challenging words, several of which you are learning in this text, and how many times a word has appeared in the *New York Times* in the past year with an example of the word in context, visit www.nytimes.com/learning/students/wordofday.

For dictionary entries, a word-of-the-day feature, and word-related games, give the Merriam-Webster Online dictionary at www.m-w.com a look.

HINT

Marking Words When Reading

When you read for fun, it can be counterproductive to stop and look up every word you don't know—you will become frustrated with reading instead of enjoying it. As this book advocates, looking for context clues is the best way to find the meaning of an unknown word, but sometimes this method doesn't work. There are various ways of keeping track of unfamiliar words; try these methods to see which fits your style.

- Keep a piece of paper and a pen next to you, and write down the word and page number.
- Keep a piece of paper next to you, and rip it into small pieces or use sticky notes. Put a piece between the pages where the word you don't know is located. For added help, write the word on the paper.
- If the book belongs to you, circle the words you don't know and flip through the book later to find them.
- If the book belongs to you, dog-ear the page (turn the corner down) where the word you don't know is located. This method is useful when you don't have paper or a pen handy.
- Repeat the word and page number to yourself a few times. Try to connect the page number to a date to help you remember it.

When you are done reading for the day, get your dictionary and look up the words you marked. The last two methods work best if you don't read many pages before you look up the words or if there are only a few words you don't know. Using these methods will help you learn new words without damaging the fun of reading. Note: If you come across a word you don't know several times and not knowing its meaning hinders your understanding of what is going on, then it's a good idea to stop and look up the word.

Focus on Chapters 13–17

The following activities give you a chance to interact some more with the vocabulary words you've been learning. By looking at art, taking tests, answering questions, doing a crossword puzzle, and working with others, you will see which words you know well and which you still need to work with.

Art

Match each picture below to one of the following vocabulary words. Use each word once.

VOCABULARY LIST

visualization	multitude	connoisseur
affluence	hail	ominous

1. _____

2. _____

3. _____

4. _____

5. _____

6. _____

1 Pick the word that best completes each sentence.

1. Brushing my teeth and flossing have been part of my nightly _____ since I was a kid.

   a. annals   b. ritual   c. montage   d. anecdote

2. I thought it was _____ of Jenna not to invite me to her party, but my mother said it wasn't such a big deal.

   a. relevant   b. surreal   c. heinous   d. nomadic

3. The speaker's _____ gave me a chance to see whether I had written down all the major points he had made.

   a. juxtaposition   b. multitude   c. artifact   d. summation

4. The _____ in the movie brought out the rich green colors of the Irish countryside.

   a. affluence   b. hierarchy   c. manifest   d. cinematography

5. Because my grandmother is saving her doll collection for _____, I wasn't allowed to play with the dolls when I was little.

   a. genre   b. posterity   c. summation   d. hierarchy

2 Complete the following sentences using the vocabulary words. Use each word once.

a. verity	b. testimony	c. hierarchy	d. annals	e. juxtaposition

1. Because the man tended to mumble throughout his _____, no one on the jury believed what he said.

2. The _____ of the painting of the starving man next to the one of the king in his finery helped to show why the French were upset with the aristocracy.

3. The _____ of the candidate's statements was called into question the next day when the newspaper printed an article with completely different statistics than had been given at the town hall meeting the night before.

4. When they added two more levels to the _____ at work, people got confused about who they should report to.

5. In the _____ of history, Cleopatra, Queen Elizabeth I, and Catherine the Great will go down as three powerful female leaders.

3 Finish the story using the vocabulary words. Use each word once.

VOCABULARY LIST

procure	anecdote	attuning	manifest	quell	disconcerted
wane	relevant	nomadic	surreal	viable	ramification

The Good Old Days

My life has seemed a bit (1)_____ these last few days.
It all started with a dream that I was a kid again playing ball
and hanging out with my friends. But I was also part of a(n)
(2)_____ group that traveled the world looking for
food. Wherever we stopped, we would (3)_____ a
basket of groceries from a local market. I can't remember all of
the kinds of food we got, but I do remember cookies, ice
cream, and cheese sticks. For some reason my brain didn't
want to (4)_____ my problem in a clear way, so I was
going to have to figure out what the dream meant.

To help my (5)_____ mind calm down, I decided
to take a walk. The walk didn't (6)_____ my uneasy feelings when one of the first things I heard
was the sound of an ice cream truck. Suddenly more childhood memories flooded my brain. I felt that these
dreams and memories had to have some kind of (7)_____ for my life, but what? I then remembered seeing kids eating ice cream cones in the park the other day and thinking that they sure looked like
they were having fun. Also a friend recently told me a(n) (8)_____ about the delicious soft serve
ice cream he would get at a stand on the beach as a kid. Those lazy summer days he described just don't
seem (9)_____ to me anymore. I always seem to have something to do between work and school.
Maybe that is why I was thinking about the past so much—I was just overwhelmed by the present.

Two days later, my interest in my dream had begun to (10)_____. I was on my way to work
and (11)_____ myself to life in the present when I drove around the corner and saw a Dreamy
Ice Cream Parlor on Main Street. It must have just opened. I hadn't been in one since I was nine. All the
ice cream dreams, images, and stories now seemed (12)_____ to my present life. I quickly decided to call in late for work and make the time to relive the good old days or my brain would never rest.

Answer the following questions to further test your understanding of the vocabulary words.

1. On what activity would you like to levy a fee?

_____

2. If someone was making derogatory statements about a good friend of yours, what would you say to the person?

_____

3. Are you the kind of person who can throw an impromptu party? Explain why or why not.

_____

_____

4. Name two situations where levity would be appropriate.

_____

_____

5. Name two places you might find an artifact.

_____

_____

6. Name a belief or idea you are immutable about.

_____

7. What is your favorite genre to read?

_____

8. What are two traits that epitomize an excellent student?

_____

_____

9. What are three ideas or trends that the United States has exported?

_____

_____

10. Name a job people should be meticulous in doing.

_____

11. Name two qualities that lead most people to venerate someone.

_____

_____

12. What are four images that would be in a montage of your life in the past week?

_____

_____

_____

Crossword Puzzle

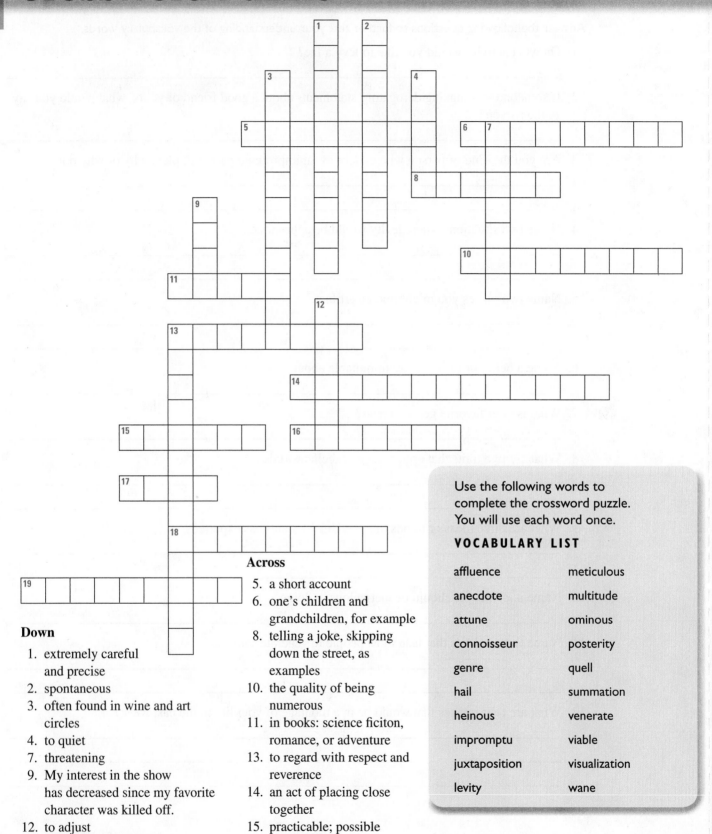

Across

5. a short account
6. one's children and grandchildren, for example
8. telling a joke, skipping down the street, as examples
10. the quality of being numerous
11. in books: science ficiton, romance, or adventure
13. to regard with respect and reverence
14. an act of placing close together
15. practicable; possible
16. wicked; evil
17. to cheer
18. wealth; an abundance
19. could begin, "In conclusion…"

Down

1. extremely careful and precise
2. spontaneous
3. often found in wine and art circles
4. to quiet
7. threatening
9. My interest in the show has decreased since my favorite character was killed off.
12. to adjust
13. the formation of mental images

Use the following words to complete the crossword puzzle. You will use each word once.

VOCABULARY LIST

affluence	meticulous
anecdote	multitude
attune	ominous
connoisseur	posterity
genre	quell
hail	summation
heinous	venerate
impromptu	viable
juxtaposition	visualization
levity	wane

Mix It Up

Category Race

Get together with a dozen classmates or so, and form three to four teams. Each team needs a set of flash cards for the words to be studied and a blank sheet of paper. Each team thinks of a category, writes it at the top of the sheet of paper, and places flash cards that fit in that category underneath the heading. Alternatively, you can write the words on the paper. After ten minutes, call time. Each group reads its category and words. There may be some disagreement on whether a word fits the category; discuss the word and its meanings to decide these issues. The team that supplies the most words wins. Another way to play is to give each team the same category and seven minutes to record its words. You can also do this activity with each person making his or her own category list. If you do it individually, you can compete with just three or four people.

Possible categories:
1. travel words
2. words that show trouble
3. health-related words
4. history words
5. love-life words
6. crime-related words
7. business-related words
8. undesirable qualities

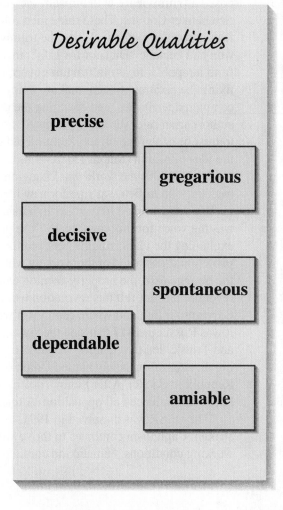

Desirable Qualities

precise

gregarious

decisive

spontaneous

dependable

amiable

Political Science

Searching for the Ideal

Political systems have come in many forms over the course of human history. The quest for a **utopian** form of government has run the **gamut** from monarchies to democracies. Ancient Rome and the Soviet Union are two examples separated by time and
5 place that show the similarities and differences in how governments are run.

Julius Caesar

After the rule of a tyrannical king, the Romans formed a **republic** around 500 B.C. The senators of the republic worked together to make decisions regarding laws. This system worked
10 well until Rome began to expand and it became harder to control the many lands Rome had conquered. Eventually military power became more important than laws. In 62 B.C. Julius Caesar proposed a **triumvirate** with himself, the general Pompey, and the rich banker Crassus. These three men ruled Rome through bribery,
15 fear, and other methods. When the triumvirate collapsed, Pompey and Caesar went to war. Caesar won and became "Dictator for Life"; there was even talk of making Caesar a king. Rome had gone from a republic to a **totalitarian** government. Caesar did make improvements for the people such as fixing the taxation system, making living conditions easier in the conquered territories, and changing the calendar. Still, his
20 authoritarian rule was not appreciated, and seeing no other way to **oust** him, a group of nobles murdered Caesar in the Senate on the Ides of March (March 15) in 44 B.C.

In the 1800s the world was changing due to the rise of industrialism. The **milieu** was ripe for new ideas. Many people lived
25 in slums and worked long hours in harsh conditions. Karl Marx was the voice for this class. In 1867 he published *Das Kapital,* explaining the class struggle between the poor and the rich. The **proletariat** consisted of the workers who could gain power from the **bourgeoisie**, the property-owning capitalist class, only by
30 revolution. Marx felt this revolution would take place in Germany or England where capitalism was well established, but it was Russia in 1917 that saw the start of communism. Lenin and Trotsky led the fight for workers' rights with Lenin becoming dictator of the newly named Union of Soviet Socialist
35 Republics (USSR). After Lenin's death in 1924, Stalin became dictator. Stalin began many reforms, but he also silenced all opposition. A totalitarian government was born again.

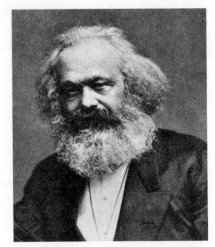

Karl Marx

The USSR was dissolved in 1991, and the ideological **underpinnings** of communism have been shaken. Capitalism continues to thrive worldwide, although workers still fight for fair wages and safe working conditions. Humankind continues its search for an ideal form of government.

Predicting

For each set, write the definition on the line next to the word to which it belongs. If you are unsure, return to the reading on page 116, and underline any context clues you find. After you've made your predictions, check your answers against the Word List on page 121. Place a checkmark in the box next to each word whose definition you missed. These are the words you'll want to study closely.

Set One

the entire range	resembling an ideal place	a government of three rulers or officials
a government that uses dictatorial control	a state where power rests with the citizens

☐   1.   **utopian** (line 2) _____

☐   2.   **gamut** (line 3) _____

☐   3.   **republic** (line 8) _____

☐   4.   **triumvirate** (line 13) _____

☐   5.   **totalitarian** (line 17) _____

Set Two

environment	foundations	the working class	to remove	the property-owning class

☐   6.   **oust** (line 21) _____

☐   7.   **milieu** (line 24) _____

☐   8.   **proletariat** (line 28) _____

☐   9.   **bourgeoisie** (line 29) _____

☐   10.   **underpinnings** (line 37) _____

Self-Tests

1 Circle the correct meaning of each vocabulary word.

1. utopian:	idealized	realized
2. republic:	power with a dictator	power with the people
3. bourgeoisie:	middle class	working class
4. triumvirate:	rule by one	rule by three
5. oust:	to remove	to add
6. gamut:	range	one and only
7. milieu:	emptiness	surroundings
8. proletariat:	working class	middle class
9. totalitarian:	liberal	authoritarian
10. underpinning:	basis	conclusion

2 Answer each question by writing the vocabulary word on the line next to the example it best fits. Use each word once.

Set One

VOCABULARY LIST

oust	triumvirate	utopian	gamut	totalitarian

1. Reginald told his bike racing team that he would order all the team's clothing in the sizes he thought people needed, and he would decide which races people would go to. What kind of leader is he? _____

2. The team decided to remove Reginald as its manager. What did it decide to do with him? _____

3. Reginald cried and then laughed when the team told him he had to go. What can be said about his emotions? _____

4. Reginald then joined with Karl and Miguel to be the leaders of a new team. What did the three of them form? _____

5. The three men feel that they will never argue with each other and that their team will win every race. What is their outlook on life? _____

Set Two

VOCABULARY LIST

bourgeoisie	republic	proletariat	milieu	underpinnings

6. Keri just bought a house by the lake. What group has she become a part of, according to Marxist theory? _____

7. Matthew rents an apartment and works as a busboy. What group does he belong to, following Marxist theory? _____

8. Keri and Matthew get to vote for the president of their country. What kind of political system does their country have? _____

9. Matthew and Keri became friends when they met in the park at a soccer game. An avid interest in sports has cemented their friendship. What is a term for the basis of a relationship? _____

10. They both work in busy places: Keri in an office and Matthew at a restaurant. What is one's environment called? _____

3 Complete the reading using each word once.

> **VOCABULARY LIST**
>
> | | | | | |
> |---|---|---|---|---|
> | underpinnings | milieu | triumvirate | utopian | bourgeoisie |
> | proletariat | oust | republic | gamut | totalitarian |

The Survey

For my political science class, I took a survey asking students what life would be like in their
(1) _____ society. I was surprised at some of the responses I got. The answers ran the
(2) _____ from governments that gave citizens complete freedom to those that had strict
control of a person's every move. I was surprised at first by the woman who favored a(n)
(3) _____ form of government, but the more I talked to her, the more I saw that she didn't like
making any kind of decision. The (4) _____ of most people's societies were freedom and
equality. Most of the students favored a(n) (5) _____ and liked the idea of citizens getting to
make decisions about laws. Most people didn't want a class society. Several students said they thought
it was unfair how the (6) _____ had manipulated workers for years. A few people even felt
that, in an ideal society, everyone would belong to the (7) _____ and work together for the
good of society, although several noted that this system hadn't been historically successful. Most people felt the (8) _____ in the perfect society would be one of peace. One man wrote on his survey, "I'd (9) _____ any whiners from my town, and then life would be great." For fun, I asked
my classmates what three people—dead or alive, real or fictional—they would pick if the government
was run as a(n) (10) _____. My favorite response was Oprah, Superman, and Princess Diana.
The survey helped me write an excellent paper on people's views of society and government.

Word Wise

Collocations

The game brought out a *gamut of emotions* from sadness and anger to eventual happiness. (Chapter 19)

Word Pairs

Bourgeoisie/Proletariat: Bourgeoisie (Chapter 19) in Marxist theory means "the property-owning
capitalist class." Proletariat (Chapter 19), also in Marxist theory, refers to "the workers who do not
own property and who must sell their labor to survive." On a Saturday afternoon, the bourgeoisie
enjoy a relaxing stroll through the park, while the proletariat continue to toil in the factories.

Interesting Etymologies

Utopian (Chapter 19): The noun Utopia comes from Greek *ou,* "not," plus *topos,* "a place" and
means "nowhere." The word was coined by Thomas More in 1516 to use as the title of his book
about an imaginary ideal island society. A utopia (lowercase) is "any ideal place," and the adjective
utopian means "resembling utopia."

Interactive Exercise ||||||||||||||||||||||||||||||||||||||||||||||||||||||||||||||||||

Give two examples for each of the following situations.

EXAMPLE: **milieu** at a sporting event   *fans cheering*   *a scoreboard flashing*

1. **milieu** at a party

2. **proletariat** actions

3. **underpinnings** of a charity

4. characteristics of a **utopian** society

5. circumstances that would cause a company to **oust** its president

6. actions of a **totalitarian** government

7. a **gamut** of emotions

8. **bourgeoisie** behavior

9. actions in a **republic**

10. where a **triumvirate** could be found

HINT

Banned Books

Freedom of expression has not always been a right granted to all people in all places. Over the centuries, several books have been banned because of their content or wording. Many of the books that are now considered classics were banned at one time. A person doesn't have to like every book that is printed, but keeping an open mind about what one is asked to read in college or what one chooses to read later in life helps to foster creativity, critical thinking, and understanding in an individual.

The following are a few books that have been banned previously (Are any a surprise to you?):

Of Mice and Men by John Steinbeck
The Catcher in the Rye by J. D. Salinger
The House of Spirits by Isabel Allende
Beloved by Toni Morrison
Lord of the Flies by William Golding

The Color Purple by Alice Walker
James and the Giant Peach by Roald Dahl
To Kill a Mockingbird by Harper Lee
Bless Me Ultima by Rudolfo Anaya
Harry Potter (the series) by J. K. Rowling

Word List

bourgeoisie
[boor′ zhwä zē′]

n. 1. in Marxist theory, the property-owning capitalist class
2. the middle class

gamut
[gam′ ət]

n. the entire scale or range

milieu
[mil yoo′]

n. environment; surroundings

oust
[oust]

v. to remove; to force out

proletariat
[prō′ li târ′ ē ət]

n. 1. in Marxist theory, the workers who do not own property and who must sell their labor to survive
2. the lowest or poorest class

republic
[ri pub′ lik]

n. 1. a state where power rests with the citizens
2. a state where the head of government is usually an elected president

totalitarian
[tō tal′ i târ′ ē ən]

adj. 1. pertaining to a government that uses dictatorial control and forbids opposition
2. authoritarian
n. an adherent of totalitarian principles or government

triumvirate
[trī um′ vər it, -və rāt′]

n. 1. a government of three rulers or officials functioning jointly
2. any group of three

underpinning
[un′ dər pin′ ing]

n. a foundation or basis (often used in the plural)

utopian
[yoo tō′ pē ən]

adj. 1. resembling utopia, an ideal place
2. involving idealized perfection
3. given to impractical schemes of perfection

Words to Watch

Which words would you like to practice with a bit more? Pick 3–5 words to study, and list them below. Write the word and its definition, and compose your own sentence using the word correctly. This extra practice could be the final touch to learning a word.

	Word	Definition	Your Sentence
1.			
2.			
3.			
4.			
5.			

Look Deeply

Poetry is an enduring form of literature because it touches people's hearts and minds as it deals with universal themes, such as love, death, and nature. However, many people also suffer from **metrophobia**, a fear of poetry. What often scares
5 people about poetry is its **ambiguous** nature. A poem doesn't always have one clear meaning. It can have several possible meanings, which can be intimidating, but it can also be the joy of poetry because it can be discussed, delighted in, and reflected on in numerous ways.

10   The **foremost** Scottish poet Robert "Bobby" Burns (1759–1796) shows how the theme of love can be imaginatively dealt with in verse in his poem "A Red, Red Rose." He wrote:

> O My Luve's like a red, red rose,
>   That's newly sprung in June;
15 O My Luve's like the melodie
>   That's sweetly played in tune.

Comparisons using *like* or *as* are called **similes**. They are an effective way to get a reader to make a connection between two distinct things. In this case, Burns compares love to a rose and to music. Burns could have used a **metaphor** such as, "My luve is a rose." The direct comparison of an object with something
20 that is usually not associated with it also helps the reader see the object in a new way. Also important in "A Red, Red Rose" is the **imagery**. It is how readers come to feel a poem. Burns tries to get the reader to use his or her senses to feel the speaker's love. He wants the reader to see and smell the rose and hear the tune to understand the power of love.

    Another important **motif** in poetry is death. A writer who tackled this subject was Emily
25 Dickinson (1830–1886). Dickinson was a recluse who rarely saw anyone for most of her life. All but seven of her almost fifteen hundred poems were published **posthumously**. In her poem "Because I Could Not Stop for Death" she uses **personification** by giving death a carriage in which to pick up the speaker: "He [Death] kindly stopped for me—/The carriage held but just Ourselves." Giving an inanimate object human characteristics can help a reader identify with the subject of the poem.

30   To overcome one's metrophobia, it is important to appreciate that it is often through **inference** that readers come to understand a poem. Poets don't always come right out and tell the reader what they mean. For instance, in her poem "A Song in the Front Yard," American poet Gwendolyn Brooks (1917–2000) seems to be talking about her yard:

> I've stayed in the front yard all my life.
35 I want a peek at the back
> Where it's rough and untended and hungry weed grows.
> A girl gets sick of a rose.

The reader now has to be willing to do some reasoning to figure out possible meanings. The front yard certainly seems to mean more than just a yard, but what does it mean? The rose and all its

40 connotations faces the reader again, and he or she needs to decide what it stands for this time. Though carefully looking at a poem can be challenging because of the language or format used, it is this effort to understand that makes poetry so enriching for readers.

Predicting ||||||||||||||||||||||||||||||||||||||||||||||||||||||||||||||||||||||||||||||||

For each set, write the definition on the line next to the word to which it belongs. If you are unsure, return to the reading on page 122, and underline any context clues you find. After you've made your predictions, check your answers against the Word List on page 127. Place a checkmark in the box next to each word whose definition you missed. These are the words you'll want to study closely.

Set One

| first in importance | a fear of poetry | open to several possible meanings |
| comparisons introduced by *like* or *as* | | a comparison between things that are not literally alike |

❑   1.   **metrophobia** (line 4) _____

❑   2.   **ambiguous** (line 5) _____

❑   3.   **foremost** (line 10) _____

❑   4.   **similes** (line 17) _____

❑   5.   **metaphor** (line 19) _____

Set Two

| the dominant theme in a work of art | mental pictures | occurring after death |
| the act of drawing a conclusion | | the act of giving human qualities to inanimate objects |

❑   6.   **imagery** (line 21) _____

❑   7.   **motif** (line 24) _____

❑   8.   **posthumously** (line 26) _____

❑   9.   **personification** (line 27) _____

❑ 10.   **inference** (line 30) _____

Self-Tests ||||||||||||||||||||||||||||||||||||||||||||||||||||||||||||||||||||||||||||||

1 For each set, match the vocabulary word to the words that could be associated with it.

SET ONE

_____ 1. posthumously	a. comparison, direct	
_____ 2. imagery	b. fear, poems	
_____ 3. metrophobia	c. senses, descriptions	
_____ 4. metaphor	d. multiple, unclear	
_____ 5. ambiguous	e. death, authors	

SET TWO

_____ 6. inference   f. human, perfect

_____ 7. foremost   g. compares, like or as

_____ 8. personification   h. reasoning, evidence

_____ 9. motif   i. top, leading

_____ 10. simile   j. main, recurring

2 Match each word to the appropriate example.

VOCABULARY LIST

foremost	simile	imagery	ambiguous	metrophobia
inference	motifs	metaphor	posthumously	personification

1. His smile is a bolt of lightning. _____

2. Her first novel was printed fifty years after her death. _____

3. "I'm afraid to read Whitman's poem _Leaves of Grass_." _____

4. The tree's branches spread over me like a fortress. _____

5. The walls shook with laughter, the ceiling had a wide grin, and the floors just smiled; the house knew my cleaning wouldn't last a day. _____

6. I bit into the large, cream cheese–frosted, freshly baked cinnamon roll; listened to the screams from the midway rides; and felt the warm sun on my back—it was good to be at the county fair. _____

7. Yesterday was the change to daylight saving time, and John, who is usually prompt, is forty minutes late. He probably forgot to change his clock. _____

8. Nature's beauty, lost love, and patriotism are a few common ones. _____

9. The unexpected phone message: "Pick me up at the airport at 8 tomorrow." _____

10. William Shakespeare as a playwright and poet, and Beethoven in music. _____

3 Finish the sentences using the vocabulary words. Use each word once.

VOCABULARY LIST

metrophobia	ambiguous	imagery	simile	foremost
personification	metaphor	motif	inference	posthumously

1. Kafka didn't want his writing published _____, so he asked his friend to destroy all of his remaining work.

2. Time is an important _____ in many of Edgar Allan Poe's works.

3. The main character's answer about where he had been last night was _____. Without a clear explanation of his activities, he became a prime suspect in the inspector's investigation of the murder.

4. In "A Birthday," Christina Rossetti writes, "My heart is like an apple tree/Whose boughs are bent with thick set fruit." The _____ shows how fulfilled the speaker is because she has found love.

5. My friend compared himself to a battleship. That _____ fits him because he loves conflict.

6. Robert Frost is one of the _____ American poets.

7. William Carlos Williams uses _____ to help the reader see the wheelbarrow. He describes it as being red and "glazed with rain/water/beside the white/chickens."

8. *The Wonderful Wizard of Oz* uses _____ when the tree yells at Dorothy for picking one of its apples.

9. When the woman in the story said her husband wouldn't be coming to dinner, the reader had to make a(n) _____ because no direct reason for his disappearance was given.

10. Because some poets use many historical and literary references, their poems can be hard to understand, which has led to _____ for many people.

Word Wise

Context Clue Mini-Lesson 5

This lesson combines the techniques you have practiced in the four previous context clue mini-lessons. You will be looking for synonyms, antonyms, examples, and general meaning to help you understand the underlined words. In the paragraph below, circle any clues you find and then write the types of clues and your definitions on the lines next to the words that follow the paragraph.

The severe winter weather had kept me inside for the last three weeks. In the last few days, the storms had become sporadic. Since the snowfall was no longer constant, I thought I had a chance to get out. I came up with the preposterous idea of walking to my friend's house four miles away. It was ridiculous to think that I could get that far in the cold with snow still covering much of the area, but I headed out. For the first few blocks, I savored the smell of the fresh air and the beauty of the snow-covered trees. But after another two blocks, the snow returned, and I quickly turned around.

Type of Context Clue and Your Definition

1. Severe _____

2. Sporadic _____

3. Preposterous _____

4. Savored _____

Interactive Exercise

Write a poem about love, death, or nature using four of the following elements: imagery, metaphor, motif, personification, or simile. Don't let metrophobia get in the way. You don't have to write a great poem; this is just a chance to practice using the vocabulary words.

HINT

Tips for Enjoying Literature

Readers enjoy a book more when they become involved with it. Try to put yourself in a novel or short story by imagining yourself in a character's situation. What would you do if you had to stop an alien invasion, cope with a broken heart, or solve a murder? Learn to appreciate the descriptions of the places in the story. Try to visualize yourself hiking through the jungle, cooking a big meal in the kitchen, or hiding under a bed. Look for the author's message as you read. Ask yourself what point the author is trying to get across. Do you agree or disagree with the author's point? By putting yourself in a work of literature and thinking about the significance of events, you will want to keep reading to see what happens to the characters because now they and their world are a part of you.

Word List

ambiguous
[am big′ yoō əs]

adj. 1. open to several possible meanings or interpretations
2. difficult to understand; unclear; indistinct

foremost
[fôr′ mōst]

adj. first in importance, place, or time; chief

imagery
[im′ ij rē]

n. the use of vivid descriptions to make mental pictures; mental images

inference
[in′ fər əns]

n. the act of drawing a conclusion from evidence

metaphor
[met′ ə fôr′, -fər′]

n. a figure of speech that makes a comparison between things that are not literally alike

metrophobia
[me′ trə fō′ bē ə, mē′-]

n. a fear of poetry

motif
[mō tēf′]

n. the dominant theme in a literary or musical composition; a recurring element in a work of art

personification
[pər son′ ə fi kā′ shən]

n. 1. the act of giving human qualities to ideas or inanimate objects
2. a person or thing that is the perfect example of a quality

posthumously
[pos′ choo məs lē]

adv. 1. occurring after death
2. published after the death of the author

simile
[sim′ ə lē]

n. a figure of speech that compares two unlike things, introduced by the word *like* or *as*

Words to Watch

Which words would you like to practice with a bit more? Pick 3–5 words to study, and list them below. Write the word and its definition, and compose your own sentence using the word correctly. This extra practice could be the final touch to learning a word.

Word	Definition	Your Sentence
1. _____	_____	_____
_____	_____	_____
2. _____	_____	_____
_____	_____	_____
3. _____	_____	_____
_____	_____	_____
4. _____	_____	_____
_____	_____	_____
5. _____	_____	_____
_____	_____	_____

21 Computer Science

Concerns to Consider

Technology, especially the computer, is rapidly changing the world. The **ubiquitous** nature of the computer is probably not even realized by most people. We see them in our homes, in schools, and in libraries, but computer technology can be found in cars, cell phones, and even appliances like washing machines. With the increased reliance on technology, some people are **wary** of the changes and
5 wonder if society is moving too quickly. Other people embrace the changes and look forward to the benefits of each new innovation.

One concern deals with privacy. Many people today enjoy the ease of shopping, banking, and paying bills online. However, if your personal information is not securely **encrypted**, problems can arise. Without encoding private information, unscrupulous people can access credit card numbers,
10 bank accounts, or other personal information. Your money can easily be stolen but, even worse, so can your identity. If this happens, the criminal can use your name to commit crimes from theft to murder. It can take years and loads of paperwork to get your good name back. Another area that worries some people is the idea of **embedding** computer
15 chips in clothing and possibly in a person's hand or brain. Researchers are looking at attaching global positioning systems (GPS) to jackets and putting miniature cameras into necklaces. A person could simply push buttons on one's sleeve to listen to music or text a message. One may even be able to swipe a hand
20 over a scanner to pay for a bill instead of using a credit card. The question is whether the benefits of having less to carry outweigh the possible loss of privacy. Some people can be considered **paranoid** in their concern that someone is constantly watching them; on the other hand, George Orwell's idea of Big
25 Brother, as presented in his novel *1984,* could become a reality.

Another area of concern is language. Some people are afraid that English is being corrupted by the **jargon** computers have created. New words and new ways of using words have come from computers. We now "surf" the Web and use a "mouse" to move the cursor. Abbreviations are especially popular. E-mailing and text messaging have developed shorthand languages. With the use of terms
30 like OIC (Oh, I see) and 2G2BT (too good to be true), many people feel that the English language has become unintelligible. For those who regularly use this method of communication, it is a fast and easy way to stay in touch with family and friends.

Some people have **qualms** about individuals interacting too often with computers and becoming out of touch with real people. People who **telecommute** and live alone may not see or speak to a live
35 person all week. This divide may even become greater as computers become more **humanoid**. Computer scientists are developing computers that can sense your mood. These computers would use cameras and microphones to examine facial expressions and listen to sounds. They would also use touch to see how a person handles the mouse. If the computer sensed that you were upset, it would try to cheer you up, possibly by telling a joke or sympathizing with you. If you continually pushed the
40 mouse hard, the computer might take this as a signal of frustration. The computer could then offer to

help with your problem. Many people would love a computer friend who would be readily available for support. Others have genuine concerns about isolation and the inability of people to communicate with one another.

45   What one person sees as a wonderful innovation, such as having a refrigerator that tells you that you are out of milk and eggs or offers you recipe suggestions based on what is in the refrigerator, another person sees as an infringement. Some people are afraid that the more computers can do for us the less we will

50   be able to think for ourselves. None of us can be **complacent** as we face the challenges and enjoy the benefits new technologies bring. We will all need to do more than THT (think happy thoughts) if we are to deal with the pros and cons of each new development.

Predicting

For each set, write the definition on the line next to the word to which it belongs. If you are unsure, return to the reading on page 128, and underline any context clues you find. After you've made your predictions, check your answers against the Word List on page 133. Place a checkmark in the box next to each word whose definition you missed. These are the words you'll want to study closely.

Set One

put into a code	showing unreasonable suspicion	fixing deeply into something	watchful

existing everywhere

☐ 1. **ubiquitous** (line 1) _____

☐ 2. **wary** (line 4) _____

☐ 3. **encrypted** (line 8) _____

☐ 4. **embedding** (line 14) _____

☐ 5. **paranoid** (line 23) _____

Set Two

to work from home by using a computer linked to one's company   feelings of doubt   self-satisfied

the language of a particular profession or group   resembling human beings

☐ 6. **jargon** (line 27) _____

☐ 7. **qualms** (line 33) _____

☐ 8. **telecommute** (line 34) _____

☐ 9. **humanoid** (line 35) _____

☐ 10. **complacent** (line 50) _____

1 Circle the correct meaning of each vocabulary word.

1. embed:	to implant	to extract
2. telecommute:	to work in an office	to work from home
3. humanoid:	having animal traits	having human characteristics
4. jargon:	unintelligible talk	simple language
5. ubiquitous:	existing everywhere	found nowhere
6. complacent:	worried	untroubled
7. wary:	cautious	hasty
8. encrypt:	to put into a code	to share
9. paranoid:	suspicious	trusting
10. qualm:	certainty	uneasiness

2 Complete the following sentences using the vocabulary words. Use each word once.

VOCABULARY LIST

humanoid	telecommute	encrypt	complacent	paranoid
jargon	ubiquitous	wary	embedded	qualm

1. We had become _____ about updating the security software on our computer, so we shouldn't have been surprised when a hacker attacked.

2. My major _____ about going camping this weekend is the weather. There is supposed to be a huge snowstorm in the mountains.

3. I enjoy science fiction shows with _____ characters, such as Data from *Star Trek: The Next Generation* or the Cylons in *Battlestar Galactica*.

4. The geologist carefully dug out the fossil that had been _____ in the side of the cliff for millions of years.

5. So much Internet _____ is based on abbreviations that I'm often unsure of what someone is trying to tell me.

6. My friend is _____ that someone is listening to his phone conversations, so sometimes we have to speak in code.

7. I was afraid to buy anything online because I thought my credit card number would be stolen, but after I read how carefully sites _____ information these days, I have been successfully shopping electronically for months.

8. Computer terms have become so _____ that my five-year-old said he wanted an "e-hug" from me instead of a real hug.

9. I am _____ of ads that claim to be able to make me look twenty years younger or make me rich in one month.

10. I'm glad my job lets me _____; I hated dealing with the horrible traffic every morning and evening when I had to drive to work.

3 Match each vocabulary word to the appropriate situation or example. Use each word once.

VOCABULARY LIST

wary	telecommute	encrypt	complacent	paranoid
jargon	embed	humanoid	qualm	ubiquitous

1. packing a vase in a box to ship _____
2. hard drive, CD-ROM, BFF, L8R _____
3. being able to work in one's pajamas _____
4. cell phones, .com _____
5. The Terminator _____
6. not studying for the third test of the semester because you got A's on the first two _____
7. possible feeling after riding a roller coaster _____
8. constantly looking over one's shoulder _____
9. reaction when you get an e-mail from a company you don't know _____
10. #jf4^)6*9j _____

Word Wise

Internet Activity: How Often Is It Used?

Here is an activity that will illustrate different contexts for the vocabulary words and emphasize the enormity of the Internet. Type a vocabulary word into a search engine such as Google or Yahoo. See how many times the word is found. Read through the first entries and see how the word is used. Find a Web site that seems interesting. Open it and look for the word again to see it in its full context. For example, the word *telecommute* turned up 3,440,000 results. Among the first ten entries, it was used in the contexts of how to find telecommuting jobs, companies friendly to telecommuting, and how to convince your boss to let you telecommute. Sometimes you will get a lot more results. *Thesis* turned up 51,800,000 results. You can also be surprised at how a word is used. Results for some other vocabulary words turned up the names of societies and magazine titles. Have fun seeing what is out there. Share your finds with classmates. What words did people pick to look up? Which word had the fewest results and which the most? Did anyone find an exciting site?

Your word: _____

Number of results: _____

A sample context: _____

Name of the Web site you visited: _____

Interactive Exercise ||||||||||||||||||||||||||||||||||||||||||||||||||||||||||||||||||||||||||||

Answer the following questions about the vocabulary words.

1. Do you feel that your private information is safely encrypted when you shop online or use the Internet for banking or other personal transactions? Explain why or why not.

   _____

2. What is something that is ubiquitous on your college campus?

   _____

3. What is a situation where it would be wise to be wary? _____

4. If you had a computer chip embedded in your hand, what features would you like it to provide?

   _____

5. Would you like a job where you could telecommute? Explain why or why not.

   _____

6. What would be an action of a paranoid? _____

7. What is something people shouldn't be complacent about? _____

8. What are two qualms freshmen usually have when they enter college?

   _____   _____

9. Would you prefer to own a computer that looks humanoid or one that looks like a machine? Why?

   _____

10. Give two examples of jargon you might use in a typical day. Where do the words come from (the Internet, text messaging, or your job)?

    _____

Word Part Reminder

Below are a few short exercises to help you review the word parts you have been learning. Fill in the missing word part from the list, and circle the meaning of the word part found in each sentence. Try to complete the questions without returning to the Word Parts chapter, but if you get stuck, look back at Chapter 17.

| trib | oid | multi | sequ |

1. He looked and acted so much like a human that I was shocked to learn that Nathan is an andr_____.

2. I enjoyed getting to follow the further adventures of Detective Lewis Thor in the _____el to the first novel, where he solved a murder on the Oregon coast.

3. We will give out one thousand brochures on child safety this weekend. By dis_____uting that many, we will help a lot of people.

4. There were many reasons I failed to make it to the study session, but, among my_____tude of problems, the main one was that my car wouldn't start.

Word List

complacent
[kəm plā′ sənt]
adj. pleased with oneself, often to a dangerous degree; self-satisfied; untroubled

embed
[em bed′]
v. 1. to fix deeply into something; to implant
2. to envelop or enclose

encrypt
[en kript′]
v. 1. to put into a code
2. to change a file or e-mail message by using a code so it will be meaningless to unauthorized users if intercepted while traveling over a network

humanoid
[hyōō′ mə noid′]
adj. resembling human beings; having human characteristics
n. a being with human form; an android

jargon
[jär′ gən, -gon]
n. 1. the language of a particular profession or group
2. unintelligible talk

paranoid
[par′ ə noid′]
adj. showing unreasonable or abnormal distrust or suspicion
n. one afflicted with paranoia

qualm
[kwäm, kwôm]
n. 1. a feeling of doubt or misgiving; uneasiness
2. a feeling of sickness, faintness, or nausea

telecommute
[tel′ i kə myōōt′]
n. to work from home by using a computer linked to one's company

ubiquitous
[yōō bik′ wi təs]
adj. existing or being everywhere, especially at the same time

wary
[wâr′ ē]
adj. cautious; watchful

Words to Watch

Which words would you like to practice with a bit more? Pick 3–5 words to study, and list them below. Write the word and its definition, and compose your own sentence using the word correctly. This extra practice could be the final touch to learning a word.

Word	Definition	Your Sentence
1. _____	_____	_____
2. _____	_____	_____
3. _____	_____	_____
4. _____	_____	_____
5. _____	_____	_____

Above and Below

The Australian **hinterland**, known as the Outback, is one of the harshest environments on Earth. The desert receives little rain, and summer temperatures can reach 115° F
5 (45° C), with averages around 90° F. The wonder of the region is Uluru, a huge red sandstone **monolith** that rises 1,150 feet (350 meters) above the plain. In 1872, the explorer William Gosse named the monolith
10 Ayers Rock after a South Australian politician who supported his escapades. Uluru is the Aboriginal name for the rock. The rock has

been a sacred site for the Aborigines who have lived in the area for 20,000 years. In 1985 the rock was made part of a national park, and the name of the rock was officially recognized as Uluru. The
15 word Uluru can be roughly translated as "mother of the earth." Except for the rock grouping Kata Tjuta nineteen miles away, the land around Uluru is flat, which heightens the impressive nature of the rock. The monolith is the result of 600 million years of physical forces. Though the huge rock may look **impervious** to weather conditions, wind, sand, and rain **erosion** still play a part in shaping the rock by wearing holes in its surface. The beauty of the rock needs to be appreciated throughout
20 the day. The changing light makes the rock look brown during the day, but, as the sun sets, the rock turns red, purple, and orange. Today thousands of visitors climb the rock and enjoy the tourist facilities nearby. Those with **acrophobia**, however, are discouraged from climbing the rock as the **ascent** is made by holding on to a chain link fence. Several people have had to be rescued from the rock. It has not, however, been a fear of heights that has caused more people to refrain from the climb. The
25 rock is considered a sacred site to the Aborigines, and they prefer people not to climb it. Each year more visitors are respecting their wishes.

The Grand Canyon is a marvel of nature. In its layers of rock, more than two billion years of geology are recorded. The scale of the canyon is
30 impressive. On average the canyon is one mile (1.6 km) deep, nine miles (15 km) wide, and it runs for 280 miles (450 km). Located in northern Arizona, temperatures at the Grand Canyon fluctuate from over 100° F (38° C) in the
35 summer to 0° F (−18° C) in the winter. The eight-mile **descent** on switchback trails takes one through several environments. Every 1,000 vertical feet is equal to 300 miles of southward travel. The region is an **oasis** for diverse
40 animal populations from mountain species like

bighorn sheep to desert animals like rattlesnakes. The erosive forces of the Colorado River formed the canyon. Six million years ago the river began wearing away the rocky surface at about one hundredth of an inch (2.5 mm) a year. At one point the canyon was nothing more than a **ravine**, but over millions of years the narrow valley grew. The walls of the canyon reveal the **permutations** the area has gone

45 through. Plankton fossils embedded in the rocks show that the region was once under the sea, and other layers expose the area as having been part of a mountain range. Like Uluru, the beauty of the canyon can best be valued with the changing light. The canyon rocks are usually red, but dawn gives them a gold and silver hue, and sunset turns them bright red. A portion of the canyon was made a national park in 1919, and the park gets well over a million visitors a year. Many of these visitors would surely agree

50 with the geologist Francois E. Matthes: "Whoever stands upon the brink of the Grand Canyon beholds a spectacle unrivaled on this earth."

Predicting

For each set, write the definition on the line next to the word to which it belongs. If you are unsure, return to the reading on page 134, and underline any context clues you find. After you've made your predictions, check your answers against the Word List on page 139. Place a checkmark in the box next to each word whose definition you missed. These are the words you'll want to study closely.

Set One

| a large single block of stone | incapable of being influenced | a fear of heights |
| back country | the process by which the surface of the earth is worn away | |

❑ 1. **hinterland** (line 1) _____

❑ 2. **monolith** (line 7) _____

❑ 3. **impervious** (line 18) _____

❑ 4. **erosion** (line 18) _____

❑ 5. **acrophobia** (line 22) _____

Set Two

| a narrow valley | a downward slope | a rising or climbing movement | alterations | a refuge |

❑ 6. **ascent** (line 22) _____

❑ 7. **descent** (line 36) _____

❑ 8. **oasis** (line 39) _____

❑ 9. **ravine** (line 43) _____

❑ 10. **permutations** (line 44) _____

Self-Tests

1 Put a T for true or F for false next to each statement.

_____ 1. Using a shield made of paper would make a person impervious.

_____ 2. It is dangerous for children to play near ravines.

_____ 3. One can slide down a hill during an ascent.

_____ 4. If a woman has climbed the twenty highest peaks in North America, she probably has acrophobia.

_____ 5. A teenager's bedroom can be an oasis from the stresses of school and relationships.

_____ 6. You could possibly slide down a hill during a descent.

_____ 7. New York City is considered the hinterland of the United States.

_____ 8. Usually the erosion of a mountain is easy to see on a day-to-day basis.

_____ 9. An essay can go through many permutations before a student is ready to hand it in.

_____10. A statue sitting on the corner of a person's desk could be called a monolith.

2 Match the quotation to the word it best illustrates. Use each word once.

> **VOCABULARY LIST**
>
> | | | | | |
> |---|---|---|---|---|
> | impervious | acrophobia | ravine | ascent | descent |
> | hinterland | oasis | monolith | erosion | permutations |

1. "I tried to persuade my father to let me go to the concert, but he wouldn't let me."
_____

2. "The statues on Easter Island are so impressive." _____

3. "I'm afraid to look over the side of the building. We are on the twentieth floor!"
_____

4. "This café is my lunch-hour refuge from the stresses of work." _____

5. "The wind has made the rocks into interesting shapes." _____

6. "I am going to get away this summer; I am going to the Yukon in Canada."
_____

7. "There have been so many alterations to the plan that I am not sure what time to pick up Athena."
_____

8. "His advancement in the company has been amazing. He is now a vice-president, and he was working in the mailroom just ten months ago."
_____

9. "I'm a bit afraid of going down. There are several loose rocks on the path." _____

10. "We are going to have to leap across this one."
_____

3 Circle the word that correctly completes each sentence.

1. The latest (permutation, ascent) in the City Hall redesign plan shows a swimming pool replacing a parking lot.

2. The (ascent, erosion) of the mountain took all day. We set up camp near the top just before dark.

3. I hadn't realized I suffered from (oasis, acrophobia) until we took a hot air balloon ride. I was terrified the whole ride.

4. I am excited about my vacation to the (monolith, hinterland) of the African jungle. It will be great to get away from civilization.

5. Luckily our tent was (permutation, impervious) to water because it rained all night.

6. Her (descent, ascent) into madness was quick. Last week she was fine, and this week she is convinced that she is Queen Victoria.

7. The nomads were pleased to come across the (ravine, oasis); they were getting thirsty.

8. We had to pull Conrad out of the (ravine, monolith). He wasn't looking, and he fell in.

9. The heavy rains this winter caused a lot of (erosion, descent) on the hillside.

10. The new black skyscraper has aptly been called a(n) (acrophobia, monolith). It is so massive it dominates the downtown skyline.

Word Wise

Collocations

The award had to be *given posthumously* because the ambassador died in a plane crash on her most recent peace-saving mission. (Chapter 20)

Word Pairs

Metaphor/Simile: Metaphor (Chapter 20) means "a figure of speech that makes a comparison between things that are not literally alike." A simile (Chapter 20) means "a figure of speech that compares two unlike things, introduced by the word *like* or *as*." The poet uses both a metaphor ("her eyes are diamonds") and a simile ("her cheeks are like apples") to describe the woman.

Ascent/Descent: Ascent (Chapter 22) means "a rising or climbing movement." Descent (Chapter 22) means "a downward slope." The ascent was steep and I started breathing hard, but the view from the top was worth it. I hope that the descent will be easier; maybe I can roll down part of the hill.

Interesting Etymologies

Jargon (Chapter 21): in the Middle Ages meant "twittering" and later "meaningless chatter." That meaning still applies to one of the definitions, "unintelligible talk," and likely the definition—"the language of a particular profession or group"—sounded like meaningless chatter to those not involved in that profession.

Acrophobia (Chapter 22): comes from the Greek *akros,* "at the end, the top," plus *phobia,* "fear of." Together they join to make "a fear of heights."

Interactive Exercise

Give an example for each word. The example might be where something could happen or be found. Think locally and globally.

Examples:

Monolith   *an Easter Island statue*
Permutation   *four high rises built downtown this year*

1. acrophobia _____

2. ravine _____

3. ascent _____

4. permutation _____

5. descent _____

6. oasis _____

7. erosion _____

8. monolith _____

9. hinterland _____

10. impervious _____

Conversation Starters

An excellent way to review the vocabulary words and help to make them your own is to use them when you are speaking. Gather three to five friends or classmates, and use one or more of the conversation starters below. Before you begin talking, have each person write down six of the vocabulary words he or she will use during the conversation. Share your lists with each other to check that you did not all pick the same six words. Try to cover all of the words you want to study, whether you are reviewing one, two, or more chapters.

1. What would a utopian society be like to you? Do you think it possible that humans will ever live in a utopian world? Explain why you feel this way.

2. What types of books do you like? What attracts you to these genres? Do you have a favorite author? Is there a type of literature you really don't like? Why is that?

3. How do you use computers in your everyday life? Do you see computers as being more beneficial or dangerous? Of the areas mentioned in the reading for Chapter 21, which seems the most threatening to you?

4. Would you enjoy traveling to the hinterland of some country? Would you have to overcome acrophobia or some other kind of fear in your journey? What kind of geological features are there around your town or city?

Word List

acrophobia
[ak′ rə fō′ bē ə]

n. a fear of heights

ascent
[ə sent′]

n. 1. a rising or climbing movement
2. movement upward; advancement

descent
[di sent′]

n. 1. a downward slope
2. a decline; a fall; a drop

erosion
[i rō′ zhən]

n. the process by which the surface of the earth is worn away by the action of water, winds, waves, etc.

hinterland
[hin′ ter land′]

n. back country; the remote or less developed parts of a country

impervious
[im pûr′ vē əs]

adj. 1. incapable of being injured, impaired, or influenced
2. not permitting passage

monolith
[mon′ ə lith]

n. 1. a large single block of stone
2. a column or large statue formed from a single block of stone
3. something having a uniform, massive, or inflexible character

oasis
[ō ā′ sis]

n. 1. a refuge, as from work or stress
2. a fertile area in a desert region, usually having a spring or well

permutation
[pûr′ myoo tā′ shən]

n. alteration; transformation

ravine
[rə vēn′]

n. a narrow, steep-sided valley, usually eroded by running water

Words to Watch ||||||||||||||||||||||||||||||||||||||||||||||||||||||||||||||||||||||

Which words would you like to practice with a bit more? Pick 3–5 words to study, and list them below. Write the word and its definition, and compose your own sentence using the word correctly. This extra practice could be the final touch to learning a word.

	Word	Definition	Your Sentence
1.	_____	_____	_____
2.	_____	_____	_____
3.	_____	_____	_____
4.	_____	_____	_____
5.	_____	_____	_____

Focus on Chapters 19–22

The following activities give you a chance to interact some more with the vocabulary words you've been learning. By looking at art, taking tests, answering questions, doing a crossword puzzle, and working with others, you will see which words you know well and which you still need to work with.

Art ||||||||||||||||||||||||||||||||||||||||||||||||||||||||||||||||||||||||||||||||||||||||||||||||||||||||||||||||||||||||||||||||||||||||||||||||||||

Match each picture below to one of the following vocabulary words. Use each word once.

VOCABULARY LIST

oust   ascent   personification

oasis   telecommute   triumvirate

1. _____

2. _____

3. _____

4. _____

5. _____

6. _____

Self-Tests

1 Pick the word that best completes each sentence.

1. I had no idea Rosa suffered from _____ until I began to read the poem "Gold Story" to her, and she shuddered and ran off.

   a. jargon　　　　　b. underpinning　　　　c. acrophobia　　　d. metrophobia

2. The _____ that best fits my geography class is that it's like being at a buffet; we are studying about a different country every session.

   a. oasis　　　　　b. simile　　　　　　c. paranoid　　　　d. gamut

3. Many of the characters in the new science fiction movie will be _____, but thanks to computer imaging there will also be creatures that don't look a thing like people.

   a. humanoids　　　b. metaphors　　　　c. erosions　　　　d. totalitarians

4. Once we crossed the _____ the rest of the hike was easy.

   a. qualm　　　　　b. ravine　　　　　　c. triumvirate　　　d. inference

5. Because our government is a(n) _____, it is important that everyone votes.

   a. metrophobia　　b. ascent　　　　　　c. republic　　　　d. jargon

2 Complete the following sentences using the vocabulary words. Use each word once.

a. qualms	b. paranoid	c. bourgeoisie	d. erosion	e. imagery

1. The _____ enjoy certain privileges that the working class never gets to experience.

2. The _____ in the story was so vivid that I felt like I was walking in the jungle right next to the hero.

3. I like a good deal, but I have _____ about buying a big-screen television from a store called Jack's Cheap Appliances and Other Stuff.

4. The _____ on the hillside has been so bad this winter that several homes have suffered damage due to mud slides.

5. I don't like to sound _____, but I'm sure that the woman in the purple dress has been following us for the last two hours. She is hard to miss, and she has gone in and out of every store that we have.

3 Finish the story using the vocabulary words. Use each word once.

VOCABULARY LIST

embedded	gamut	ambiguous	monoliths	motifs	underpinning
milieu	inferences	hinterlands	permutations	wary	ubiquitous

An Adventure Down South

I was (1)_____ about traveling to South America. I had never left the United States before, but the variety of sights on this trip was just too enticing. Our stops have run the (2)_____ of environments from the tropical jungles of the Amazon to the deserts of Chile. I enjoyed getting to experience the (3)_____ of several countries. Not everyone gets to explore the backcountry of an area. I was also thrilled to see the (4)_____ of Easter Island. Those huge stone statutes have always fascinated me. There is so much history (5)_____ in each of the places we have traveled, from the Incas at Machu Picchu to Eva Peron in Buenos Aires.

I can only describe the (6)_____ in each country as one of friendliness. Everyone has been so welcoming toward our group. What I was really surprised to find was how (7)_____ ice cream shops are. Every afternoon people line up at a shop that can be found on almost every corner. I have joined in too; an ice cream cone or a gelato is a wonderful treat on a hot day.

At the beginning of the trip, our instructor was rather (8)_____ about what we should focus on at each location. He told us to keep our minds open and make (9)_____ from what we saw and heard and that, as the trip unfolded, he would give us more information. Last week he asked if we had an idea about what the (10)_____ element was in the landscapes and cultures we had learned about. I said that I had noticed llama and guanaco (11)_____ in a lot of the artwork and architecture we had seen, and I had read that they symbolized survival. My instructor said that theme was related to what he was talking about. Our last stop was Iguassu Falls, located on the borders of Argentina and Brazil. Here our instructor revealed that we had been looking at (12)_____ of both the land and the people everywhere we had been. He asked us to write an essay that describes how the waterfalls symbolize those alterations. The paper will serve as a perfect summation to a glorious trip.

Interactive Exercise |||||||||||||||||||||||||||||||||||||||||||||||||||||||||||||||||||||||||||||||||||

Answer the following questions to further test your understanding of the vocabulary words.

1. Name two times when you shouldn't be complacent.

   _____   _____

2. Name a quality that would be essential in a utopian society.

   _____

3. What would you recommend a person do to see if he or she has acrophobia?

   _____

4. If you had the chance to name something in your city after a person posthumously, who would
   you pick and what would you pick (examples: a building, a park, a bridge). Why did you make
   these choices?

   _____

   _____

5. Give two examples of things a totalitarian government would do.

   _____   _____

6. Create a metaphor that compares your personality to an animal.

   _____

7. List two characteristics of the proletariat.

   _____   _____

8. What is the foremost problem at your college? What is a possible solution?

   _____

   _____

9. What are two pieces of information you would want to make sure were encrypted when you sent
   them over the Internet?

   _____   _____

10. Name an item that is supposedly impervious to destruction.

    _____

11. Which do you think is harder when climbing a mountain, the ascent or the descent? Why?

    _____

    _____

12. Give two examples of jargon from the computer, medical, legal, or other field with which you are
    familiar.

    _____   _____

Crossword Puzzle

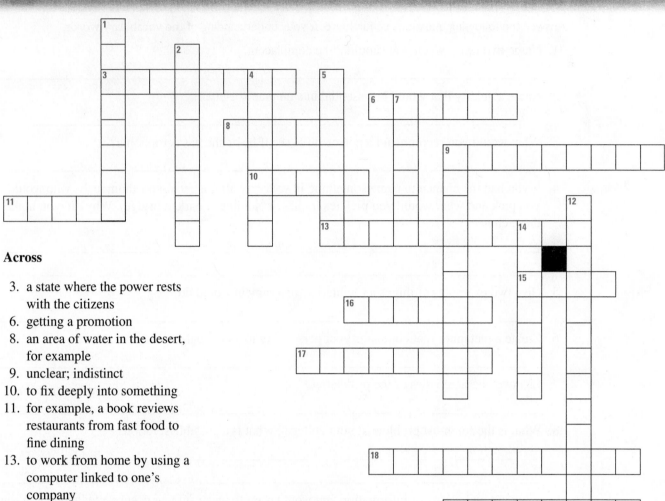

Across

3. a state where the power rests with the citizens
6. getting a promotion
8. an area of water in the desert, for example
9. unclear; indistinct
10. to fix deeply into something
11. for example, a book reviews restaurants from fast food to fine dining
13. to work from home by using a computer linked to one's company
15. to force out
16. 1DR, IMO, APB, stat
17. showing unreasonable suspicion
18. any group of three
19. a large single block of stone

Down

1. chief
2. having human characteristics
4. mental images
5. a downward slope or a decline
7. His personality is like a cactus.
9. fear of heights
12. My life is so hectic that the calendar sneers at me.
14. involving idealized perfection

Use the following words to complete the crossword puzzle. You will use each word once.

VOCABULARY LIST

acrophobia	monolith
ambiguous	oasis
ascent	oust
descent	paranoid
embed	personification
foremost	republic
gamut	simile
humanoid	telecommute
imagery	triumvirate
jargon	utopian

Mix It Up

Motivating with Music

If you enjoy music, select some of your favorite tunes and get together with four or five classmates to see how music can aid in learning. Besides the music, you will need something to play it on, paper, and pens. Decide on which words you want to study. If you are reviewing several chapters, each person should pick different vocabulary words to use so the group can cover more of the words.

While the music plays, write a story that the music inspires using six or seven of the words to be studied (you may choose to write six or seven sentences each using a vocabulary word instead of writing a story). The ideas for the story or sentences may come from the tone of the music or the thoughts expressed in a song's lyrics. Share your stories or sentences with each other, and discuss the ideas the music brought out in relation to the vocabulary words. It is interesting to hear the similarities and differences the music inspires within the group. To review more words, pick another piece of music and do the activity again.

Classical music works well, but music related to a chapter may also serve as inspiration and possibly as a memory aid. For example, use patriotic music from any country for relating to Chapter 19, love songs for Chapter 20, techno music for Chapter 21, and rock music for Chapter 22. Have fun exploring how music, writing, and learning vocabulary can be creatively combined.

24

Education

What's Your Personality?

It is obvious that people react differently in the same situations and that people have job and hobby preferences. In an effort to understand the reasons for these differences, researchers began to **classify** people's

5 behaviors into different categories called personality types. Katherine Briggs and her daughter Isabel Briggs-Myers, beginning in the 1920s, developed one of the most famous personality tests. They based their studies on the Swiss psychologist Carl Jung's

10 (1875–1961) work. Jung felt people had **inherent** preferences and that, to lead a successful life, one

needed to focus on those preferences and not try to change them. Briggs and her daughter took Jung's ideas and began to study thousands of people to come up with questions that could lead to personality profiles. By 1956 they had developed a test that the Educational Testing Service (ETS), the group that

15 administers the Scholastic Aptitude Test (SAT), was willing to publish. There was some initial resistance to the test since neither woman was a psychologist, but their work prevailed, and since then the Myers-Briggs Type Indicator (MBTI) has been given to millions of people.

One area most personality tests examine is how people prefer to interact with others. The questions aim to see whether a person is an **introvert** or **extrovert**. Introverts tend to be shy, and they do not **relish**

20 dealing with people. They prefer having a few friends to spend time with, and they like working alone. Extroverts, on the other hand, love meeting people, having lots of friends, and working with others. In school, introverts and extroverts often look at being involved in group projects differently, with extroverts usually welcoming working with others.

Another area of difference is how people perceive the world. Some people are known as "sensors."

25 They like to get information in a **sequential** order, they like facts, and they like hands-on activities. These are the people who prefer to use their five senses to gather information. They are the **tactile** people who want to touch something to test its reality. The other group is called "**intuitive**." They are fine with getting information in random order, and they enjoy dealing with

30 **abstract** ideas. In educational settings, these differences can lead to problems. Most elementary school teachers, about 70%, are sensory types, and most people are sensory types, also about 70%. The predominance of sensory early-learning teachers works well for most young students, but about 77%

35 of college professors are the intuitive type. For many sensors, a college lecture given by an intuitive, who freely makes random observations and uses generalities, becomes frustrating. They want an outline; they want order. They want concrete examples. This difference makes getting a college

40 education difficult for some personality types.

Another difference is whether people are "thinkers" or "feelers" when they make decisions. Thinkers are very logical. They tend to be detached, and their goal is fairness. Feelers are more concerned with how the results of a decision will affect other people. They are concerned with harmony over justice. The last type of difference features the "judgers" and the "perceivers." Judgers like an orderly environment. They
45 make a plan and stick to it. Perceivers prefer to be spontaneous. They don't like to make firm decisions. For this type, what works one day might not be the right thing to do the next day.

The MBTI asks questions that help people create a personality profile that includes the four ways of interacting with the world. Two possible personality types are the ISTJ (Introvert, Sensor, Thinker, Judger) and the ENFP (Extrovert, Intuitive, Feeler, Perceiver). These two types deal with situations
50 differently, and they relate to each other differently, which can sometimes lead to arguments and stressful situations. It can be helpful to understand these differences to better get along with each other and to better know oneself. Personality profiles don't try to confine the individual. They allow for the **multifaceted** nature of each person, but they can help a person see one's preferences. An awareness of why one behaves a certain way can assist a person in a variety of life's activities from
55 education and career choices to romance and money management.

Predicting

For each set, write the definition on the line next to the word to which it belongs. If you are unsure, return to the reading on page 146, and underline any context clues you find. After you've made your predictions, check your answers against the Word List on page 151. Place a checkmark in the box next to each word whose definition you missed. These are the words you'll want to study closely.

Set One

| innate | to enjoy | to organize | an outgoing person | a shy person |

☐ 1. **classify** (line 4) _____

☐ 2. **inherent** (line 10) _____

☐ 3. **introvert** (line 19) _____

☐ 4. **extrovert** (line 19) _____

☐ 5. **relish** (line 19) _____

Set Two

| pertaining to the sense of touch | | an idea not related to a specific example |
| many-sided | in order | instinctive |

☐ 6. **sequential** (line 25) _____

☐ 7. **tactile** (line 26) _____

☐ 8. **intuitive** (line 28) _____

☐ 9. **abstract** (line 30) _____

☐ 10. **multifaceted** (line 53) _____

1 Match each term with its synonym in Set One and its antonym in Set Two.

SYNONYMS

ANTONYMS

Set One

Set Two

_____ 1. intuitive   a. concrete   _____ 6. abstract   f. simple

_____ 2. classify   b. innate   _____ 7. extrovert   g. extrovert

_____ 3. tactile   c. perceptive   _____ 8. multifaceted   h. concrete

_____ 4. relish   d. enjoy   _____ 9. sequential   i. random

_____ 5. inherent   e. sort   _____ 10. introvert   j. introvert

2 Finish the following sentences. Use each word once.

VOCABULARY LIST				
introvert	relish	inherent	abstract	extrovert
multifaceted	classify	tactile	sequential	intuitive

1. An extreme _____ might spend a year alone and not miss the company of other people.

2. In a recent announcement, the mayor declared that she will _____ the task of rejuvenating the decaying downtown shopping area.

3. A study was just published that suggests kindness is _____ in all people.

4. A local professor's _____ ideas on time travel have won him a Science Foundation award.

5. My husband is the _____ in the family. He can visit with people for hours, while I prefer to sit in the corner reading a book.

6. The organization has decided to _____ most of the personal information it has about its members. From now on, only executive board members will be allowed access to this material.

7. Kids love the new _____ display at the Children's Museum. It lets them touch objects found in rivers and oceans.

8. The city council's _____ plan to restructure the city's departments will begin in departments starting with "A" and continue in order through the alphabet.

9. Audiences will be impressed with the _____ skills of Gerry the Juggler. He can sing, dance, and tell jokes all while juggling a dozen objects at one time.

10. A local musician and legend credits his productive song-writing career to his _____ nature. He feels his sensitivity has allowed him to transform people's feelings into music.

3 For each set, complete the analogies. See Completing Analogies on page 4 for instructions and p

Set One

VOCABULARY LIST

classify   inherent   relish   introvert   intuitive

1. faulty : flawed :: innate : _____
2. likes big parties : extrovert :: avoids crowds : _____
3. photographer : shoot :: librarian : _____
4. losing : disappointment :: _____ : insights
5. comedy : laugh :: dessert : _____

Set Two

VOCABULARY LIST

sequential   multifaceted   abstract   extrovert   tactile

6. sunset : visual :: a shower : _____
7. troll : mean :: _____ : sociable
8. cow : animal :: economic problems : _____
9. yell : whisper :: _____ : random
10. barber : cut :: dentist : _____

Word Wise

A Different Approach: The Story Behind the Picture

Equipment needed: Paper, pens, and pictures (postcards, family photographs, ads, or pictures from magazines)

This activity is good for visual learners and for those who like to write. It can be done in groups of three to four people or individually. Each small group selects a picture from the ones people have brought. The group writes a short (one- to two-paragraph) story for the picture. Use four to six of the vocabulary words you are studying in the story. If you are doing the activity individually, write your own story using four to six of the vocabulary words in the story. Share the picture and story with the other groups. After the sharing, choose another picture, and play another round. After two or three rounds, discuss how the same picture produces different stories and different uses of the words.

actice.

...e an example of how it could apply to a situation in college.

carrying ten books home from the library

...rent   _joining the school chorus to use the excellent voice one was born with_

. tactile   _____

2. abstract   _____

3. classify   _____

4. inherent   _____

5. extrovert   _____

6. introvert   _____

7. sequential   _____

8. intuitive   _____

9. multifaceted   _____

10. relish   _____

HINT

A World of Words

Keep your eyes open for new words. You will certainly encounter new words in the textbooks you read in college and in the lectures your professors give, but new words can be found everywhere. Don't turn off your learning when you leave the classroom. When you see a new word in a newspaper or a newsletter or even on a poster downtown, use the strategies you have learned in this book: look for context clues around the new word, try to predict the meaning, and check the dictionary if you aren't sure of the meaning. No matter where you are or at what age you may be, your vocabulary can continue to grow.

Word List

abstract
[adj. and v.
ab strakt′,
ab′ strakt,
n. ab′ strakt]

adj. 1. an idea not related to a specific example
2. not easily understood; complex
v. 1. to take out; to extract
2. to summarize; to condense
n. a summary

classify
[klas′ ə fī′]

v. 1. to organize; to categorize; to sort
2. to limit information to approved people

extrovert
[ek′ strə vûrt′]

n. an outgoing person

inherent
[in hēr′ ənt, -her′]

adj. existing in someone or something as a permanent quality; innate

introvert
[in′ trə vûrt′]

n. a shy person

intuitive
[in tōō′ i tiv]

adj. instinctive; perceptive; sensitive

multifaceted
[mul′ tē fas′ i tid, tī-]

adj. many-sided; versatile; complex

relish
[rel′ ish]

v. 1. to enjoy; to take pleasure in
2. to like the taste of
n. pleasurable appreciation of anything; liking

sequential
[si kwen′ shəl]

adj. characterized by a regular order of parts; in order; following

tactile
[tak′ til, -tīl]

adj. pertaining or perceptible to the sense of touch; concrete

Words to Watch

Which words would you like to practice with a bit more? Pick 3–5 words to study, and list them below. Write the word and its definition, and compose your own sentence using the word correctly. This extra practice could be the final touch to learning a word.

Word	Definition	Your Sentence
1. _____	_____	_____
_____	_____	_____
2. _____	_____	_____
_____	_____	_____
3. _____	_____	_____
_____	_____	_____
4. _____	_____	_____
_____	_____	_____
5. _____	_____	_____
_____	_____	_____

...ys Something New

...t world has steadily been moving away from the more
...stic sculptures and paintings of the Greek, Roman, and
...naissance artists. Starting in the 1800s, especially with
...e Impressionists, artists began to create works that were
more **emblematic** of items than actually having to look like
them. The Impressionists wanted their paintings to be
evocative of a certain mood or time of day. They played
with light in order to suggest a feeling about the scene they
captured. Their style was not always appreciated at the time,
10 but they have become **perennial** favorites with museum go-
ers and collectors. In this exhibition, you will find several
works by Impressionists including Monet, Manet, Pissarro,
Renoir, and Morisot.

Claude Monet (1840–1926), *White Waterlilies,*
Pushkin Museum of Fine Arts, Moscow.
Copyright Scala/Art Resource, NY

We also feature the Post-Impressionist Vincent van
15 Gogh (1853–1890) in his own gallery. He used many of
the techniques he learned from the Impressionists, but his
real concern was with the moods certain colors convey.
The vivid yellows he uses in many of his paintings suggest a world filled with energy, sometimes
subdued by the calming greens and blues. He **eschewed** conventional techniques and used thick
20 brush strokes to make his scenes come alive. Van Gogh was a **prolific** artist creating more than
2,000 works, though he only sold one painting, *Red
Vineyard at Arles,* bought by the Impressionist artist Anna
Boch. After his death, his reputation flourished. His
Portrait of Dr. Gachet, done in 1890, was auctioned for
25 $82.5 million in 1990. At the time, it was the most expen-
sive painting ever sold.

Vincent van Gogh (1853–1890), *Yellow Wheat
and Cypresses,* 1889. Oil on canvas. National
Gallery, London, Great Britain. Copyright Erich
Lessing/Art Resource, NY

Subsequent art movements have moved even further
from realistic interpretations of people and objects. Our exhibition features works by Pablo Picasso (1881–1973) that
30 show how Cubism fragmented people and objects to again
move away from realistic portrayals. The angles used in
much of Picasso's work pay **tribute** to the African masks
that inspired him. Other galleries present the surrealism of
Salvador Dali, the splatter paintings of Jackson Pollock, and
35 the Pop art of Andy Warhol to further show how abstract art
has become.

Besides paintings, we have creations by Henry Moore, Claes Oldenburg, and others in the
sculpture garden; photographs by Margaret Bourke-White and Alfred Stieglitz, among others, in
our renovated photo gallery; and Japanese tea bowls, Chinese vases, and Native American pottery

3 For each set, complete the analogies. See Completing Analogies on page 4 for instructions and practice.

Set One

VOCABULARY LIST

classify   inherent   relish   introvert   intuitive

1. faulty : flawed :: innate : _____
2. likes big parties : extrovert :: avoids crowds : _____
3. photographer : shoot :: librarian : _____
4. losing : disappointment :: _____ : insights
5. comedy : laugh :: dessert : _____

Set Two

VOCABULARY LIST

sequential   multifaceted   abstract   extrovert   tactile

6. sunset : visual :: a shower : _____
7. troll : mean :: _____ : sociable
8. cow : animal :: economic problems : _____
9. yell : whisper :: _____ : random
10. barber : cut :: dentist : _____

Word Wise

A Different Approach: The Story Behind the Picture

Equipment needed: Paper, pens, and pictures (postcards, family photographs, ads, or pictures from magazines)

This activity is good for visual learners and for those who like to write. It can be done in groups of three to four people or individually. Each small group selects a picture from the ones people have brought. The group writes a short (one- to two-paragraph) story for the picture. Use four to six of the vocabulary words you are studying in the story. If you are doing the activity individually, write your own story using four to six of the vocabulary words in the story. Share the picture and story with the other groups. After the sharing, choose another picture, and play another round. After two or three rounds, discuss how the same picture produces different stories and different uses of the words.

Interactive Exercise ||||||||||||||||||||||||||||||||||||||||||||||||||||||||

For each word, give an example of how it could apply to a situation in college.

EXAMPLES:

tactile   carrying ten books home from the library

inherent   joining the school chorus to use the excellent voice one was born with

1. tactile _____

2. abstract _____

3. classify _____

4. inherent _____

5. extrovert _____

6. introvert _____

7. sequential _____

8. intuitive _____

9. multifaceted _____

10. relish _____

Word List

abstract
[adj. and v.
ab strakt′,
ab′ strakt,
n. ab′ strakt]

adj. 1. an idea not related to a specific example
2. not easily understood; complex

v. 1. to take out; to extract
2. to summarize; to condense

n. a summary

classify
[klas′ ə fī′]

v. 1. to organize; to categorize; to sort
2. to limit information to approved people

extrovert
[ek′ strə vûrt′]

n. an outgoing person

inherent
[in hēr′ ənt, -her′]

adj. existing in someone or something as a permanent quality; innate

introvert
[in′ trə vûrt′]

n. a shy person

intuitive
[in too′ i tiv]

adj. instinctive; perceptive; sensitive

multifaceted
[mul′ tē fas′ i tid, tī-]

adj. many-sided; versatile; complex

relish
[rel′ ish]

v. 1. to enjoy; to take pleasure in
2. to like the taste of

n. pleasurable appreciation of anything; liking

sequential
[si kwen′ shəl]

adj. characterized by a regular order of parts; in order; following

tactile
[tak′ til, -tīl]

adj. pertaining or perceptible to the sense of touch; concrete

Words to Watch

Which words would you like to practice with a bit more? Pick 3–5 words to study, and list them below. Write the word and its definition, and compose your own sentence using the word correctly. This extra practice could be the final touch to learning a word.

Word	Definition	Your Sentence
1. _____	_____	_____
2. _____	_____	_____
3. _____	_____	_____
4. _____	_____	_____
5. _____	_____	_____

25

Art History

Always Something New

The art world has steadily been moving away from the more
realistic sculptures and paintings of the Greek, Roman, and
Renaissance artists. Starting in the 1800s, especially with
the Impressionists, artists began to create works that were
5 more **emblematic** of items than actually having to look like
them. The Impressionists wanted their paintings to be
evocative of a certain mood or time of day. They played
with light in order to suggest a feeling about the scene they
captured. Their style was not always appreciated at the time,
10 but they have become **perennial** favorites with museum go-
ers and collectors. In this exhibition, you will find several
works by Impressionists including Monet, Manet, Pissarro,
Renoir, and Morisot.

Claude Monet (1840–1926), *White Waterlilies,*
Pushkin Museum of Fine Arts, Moscow.
Copyright Scala/Art Resource, NY

   We also feature the Post-Impressionist Vincent van
15 Gogh (1853–1890) in his own gallery. He used many of
the techniques he learned from the Impressionists, but his
real concern was with the moods certain colors convey.
The vivid yellows he uses in many of his paintings suggest a world filled with energy, sometimes
subdued by the calming greens and blues. He **eschewed** conventional techniques and used thick
20 brush strokes to make his scenes come alive. Van Gogh was a **prolific** artist creating more than
2,000 works, though he only sold one painting, *Red
Vineyard at Arles,* bought by the Impressionist artist Anna
Boch. After his death, his reputation flourished. His
Portrait of Dr. Gachet, done in 1890, was auctioned for
25 $82.5 million in 1990. At the time, it was the most expen-
sive painting ever sold.

   Subsequent art movements have moved even further
from realistic interpretations of people and objects. Our exhibition features works by Pablo Picasso (1881–1973) that
30 show how Cubism fragmented people and objects to again
move away from realistic portrayals. The angles used in
much of Picasso's work pay **tribute** to the African masks
that inspired him. Other galleries present the surrealism of
Salvador Dali, the splatter paintings of Jackson Pollock, and
35 the Pop art of Andy Warhol to further show how abstract art
has become.

Vincent van Gogh (1853–1890), *Yellow Wheat
and Cypresses,* 1889. Oil on canvas. National
Gallery, London, Great Britain. Copyright Erich
Lessing/Art Resource, NY

   Besides paintings, we have creations by Henry Moore, Claes Oldenburg, and others in the
sculpture garden; photographs by Margaret Bourke-White and Alfred Stieglitz, among others, in
our renovated photo gallery; and Japanese tea bowls, Chinese vases, and Native American pottery

40 in the ceramics gallery. And don't miss the varied **hues** found in
the textile gallery. The reds, purples, oranges, and blues quickly
attract viewers to the rugs, quilts, scarves, and clothing from
such varied places as Central America, Morocco, and India.

   The goal of this exhibition is to show that the **essence** of art is
45 a love of diverse styles, so be sure not to miss the two galleries
devoted to new local artists. As we looked through their
portfolios, we found that their work has been inspired by a range
of styles and periods including Egyptian wall paintings, Chinese
landscapes, Mexican murals, and a multitude of modern art
50 movements. Innovations and combinations of past artistic styles
are what keep art exciting and keep the public from becoming
complacent. We want you to feel like you will never know what
you might encounter the next time you enter the museum. Please
enjoy the eclectic display we have organized for your enjoyment
55 this spring.

Predicting ||||||||||||||||||||||||||||||||||||||||||||||||||||||||||||||||||||||||||||||||||||||||||||||||||||||

For each set, write the definition on the line next to the word to which it belongs. If you are unsure,
return to the reading on page 152, and underline any context clues you find. After you've made your
predictions, check your answers against the Word List on page 157. Place a checkmark in the box next to
each word whose definition you missed. These are the words you'll want to study closely.

Set One

symbolic	lasting through many years	creating abundant works	suggestive	avoided

☐ 1. **emblematic** (line 5) _____

☐ 2. **evocative** (line 7) _____

☐ 3. **perennial** (line 10) _____

☐ 4. **eschewed** (line 19) _____

☐ 5. **prolific** (line 20) _____

Set Two

colors	following or coming after	portable cases for holding loose sheets of paper or drawings
the crucial element	something given or done to show one's admiration	

☐ 6. **subsequent** (line 27) _____

☐ 7. **tribute** (line 32) _____

☐ 8. **hues** (line 40) _____

☐ 9. **essence** (line 44) _____

☐ 10. **portfolios** (line 47) _____

1 In each group, circle the word that does not have a connection to the other three words.

1. symbolic	direct	emblematic	representative
2. edge	spirit	essence	core
3. hue	color	tint	bare
4. case	folder	warehouse	portfolio
5. perennial	recurring	lasting	occasional
6. eschew	avoid	escape	join
7. disrespect	tribute	honor	admiration
8. following	succeeding	preceding	subsequent
9. fertile	blocked	prolific	productive
10. evocative	suggestive	summon	stated

2 Complete the following quotations overheard in art museums around the world. Use each word once.

VOCABULARY LIST

emblematic	essence	hues	portfolio	perennial
subsequent	eschew	evocative	tribute	prolific

1. "I like how so many of the works in the modern art section pay _____ to the past. Even the giant plastic banana and grapes show an appreciation of the traditional still-life painting."

2. "Georgia O'Keeffe has been a(n) _____ favorite of mine. I love how her glorious flower paintings present the beauty of nature."

3. "Diego Rivera's mural gave me a great perspective on the struggles Mexico has experienced, and I was impressed to learn how _____ artists have continued to explore the possibilities of the mural to tell about historical events."

4. "If I were an artist, I would do miniature paintings, so that they would be easy to fit into my _____."

5. "I know Picasso was trying to _____ traditional forms in his paintings, but I cannot see a woman on that staircase."

6. "The African mask exhibit was _____ of how we often hide who we are."

7. "Dali's paintings really capture the _____ of the dream world."

Georgia O'Keeffe (1887–1986), *White Flower on Red Earth, #1,* 1943. Oil on canvas, 26 in. × 30 1/4 in. Collection of the Newark Museum, Newark, New Jersey. Copyright The Newark Museum/Art Resource, NY. © 2002 The Georgia O'Keeffe Foundation/Artists Rights Society (ARS), New York

8. "The pink and purple _____ in Suzanne Valadon's *Lilacs and Peonies* show the delicacy of spring."

9. "I hadn't realized how _____ Claude Monet was. He did more than two thousand paintings, and he certainly liked to do a lot of his garden, especially of the pond."

10. "I found the Hiroshige print of the rain shower to be quite _____; I could feel myself in a downpour."

3 Put a T for true or F for false next to each sentence.

_____ 1. To make sure that one's investments are doing well, a person should have an annual review of his or her portfolio.

_____ 2. An artist who creates one painting every ten years could be called prolific.

_____ 3. Nature has been a perennial subject matter for art and poetry.

_____ 4. Flags are emblematic of a country.

_____ 5. Tie-dye shirts are evocative of the 1960s.

_____ 6. A popular hue for buildings is lime green.

_____ 7. Most people would eschew the offer of a free plane ticket.

_____ 8. Several nations pay a tribute to Canada for protection.

_____ 9. Subsequent generations want to demonstrate their skills in various fields including art, music, sports, and politics.

_____ 10. The essence of doing well in school is studying.

Word Wise

Collocations

Putting a process in *sequential order* makes it easier to understand how to do it. (Chapter 24)

For Sue the *essence of* an excellent meal is having good friends to share it with. (Chapter 25)

The river's flooding has become a *perennial problem* that the city can no longer afford to ignore now that the population is growing and people are moving closer to the riverbanks. (Chapter 25)

The concert will *pay tribute to* the pioneers of jazz by showcasing their songs in video clips of the original artists and live performances by some of today's hottest musicians. (Chapter 25)

Connotations and Denotations

Introvert and Extrovert (Chapter 24): denotation of introvert—"a shy person"—and of extrovert—"an outgoing person." Depending on your personality type and experiences, your connotation of an introvert might be a quiet person with deep thoughts or a bore. You may see an extrovert as fun and friendly or loud and obnoxious. Picture a person for each type. What is the person doing? Did you picture someone you know? These visualizations may help you understand your connotations for each type.

Interactive Exercise ||||||||||||||||||||||||||||||||||||||||||||||||||||||||||||||||||||||

You are an art critic for the local newspaper. Use at least six of the vocabulary words to write your weekly column about the painting on the right. You can decide whether to admire the work or censure it, or do a bit of both.

_____

_____

_____

_____

_____

_____

_____

_____

Three Musicians

_____

_____

_____

_____

_____

_____

_____

_____

_____

_____

HINT

Make It Yours

An important step in learning new vocabulary is to practice using the words. When you feel comfortable with a word's definition, start using the word in your writing and conversations. If you only try to memorize the word for a test, you will likely forget it after the test. Make your acquisition of new vocabulary meaningful by using the words in everyday situations. Also try to connect the word to prior knowledge or experiences. Are there situations you have been in in which the word would be appropriate? Try to integrate the word with your life as much as possible. You will impress your friends and family and feel good about yourself as you show people what you have learned.

Word List

emblematic
[em' blə mat' ik]

adj. symbolic; representative

eschew
[es chōō']

v. to avoid; to shun; to escape

essence
[es' əns]

n. the quality of a thing that gives it its identity; the crucial element; core

evocative
[i vok' ə tiv]

adj. having the power to produce a reaction; suggestive

hue
[hyōō]

n. color; tint; shade

perennial
[pə ren' ē əl]

adj. 1. lasting through the year or through many years; everlasting
2. continually recurring

portfolio
[pôrt fō' lē ō']

n. 1. a portable case for holding loose sheets of paper or drawings
2. a list of the investments owned by a bank, investment organization, or other investor

prolific
[prō lif' ik]

adj. creating abundant works or results; plentiful; fertile

subsequent
[sub' si kwent', -kwənt']

adj. following or coming after; succeeding

tribute
[trib' yōōt]

n. 1. something given or done to show one's admiration, appreciation, or respect
2. a payment or tax made by one nation to another for protection or to show submission

Words to Watch

Which words would you like to practice with a bit more? Pick 3–5 words to study, and list them below. Write the word and its definition, and compose your own sentence using the word correctly. This extra practice could be the final touch to learning a word.

	Word	Definition	Your Sentence
1.			
2.			
3.			
4.			
5.			

Shopping Made Easier

One of a merchant's goals is to **garner consumer** confidence. Customers will spend their money if they feel comfortable in a shopping environment. There are several ways stores can be designed to better accommodate consumers' needs.

Businesses need to allow sufficient space between the aisles. Studies have found that if customers accidentally brush up against each other it **detracts** from the shopping experience. If a customer is repeatedly **jostled** while looking at a product, he or she will leave the store without making a purchase. If the retail space is **conducive** to browsing, then the customer will spend more time in the store, which usually translates to buying more. Retailers can also **attribute** greater sales to something as easy as placing shopping baskets throughout a store, not just at the entrance. Customers will buy more if they have a container for their purchases. A shopper may come into the store planning to buy one or two items and not pick up a basket. But if a few more items attract a customer's interest and a basket is nearby, the person will usually

pick up the basket and fill it. A customer is limited by having two hands. If the retailer provides a basket or cart, that limitation ceases to be a problem.

People love to use their senses when shopping. Retailers need to become **proponents** of the five senses. Obviously, a woman wants to touch a shirt before she buys it, but she wants to do the same with the sheets she will sleep on, and that's hard to do if the sheets are wrapped in plastic. Most stores don't provide a sample sheet to touch, and that's when a shopper feels it is her **prerogative** to make a small hole in the plastic so she can run her fingers over the fabric. Unfortunately, several items that people desire to touch, from silverware to paper, are packaged in ways that prevent shoppers from feeling them. A few stores have noted the popularity of offering food samples, especially for new products, but most are not taking advantage of this sensory-shopping method. Just seeing a package of the latest veggie burger in the freezer case is unlikely to excite a man, but if he is given a free taste, he may discover how good it is. More goods will be sold if people can touch, taste, smell, and hear products, as well as see them.

Another area where a retailer's business **acumen** can shine is at the checkout line. The checkout line is the customer's last encounter with a store, and it can destroy a good shopping experience. If customers have to wait too long, they will not return to a store, and they may even give up on what

they have already brought to the line. To quell the anger of the bored consumer, retailers need to make the waiting time seem shorter. A simple way to decrease waiting anxiety is to provide reading material. Grocery stores already do this with magazines at the checkout stands, but it is also **feasible** for other types of stores. Retailers can hang posters behind the cashiers announcing special events (book signings, garden talks, food demonstrations) or provide flyers of upcoming sales on a rack where customers can grab one to read while they wait. The checkout line is also a great place for impulse buying. Retailers should put racks of small items within easy reach of those waiting in line. Few people are going to get out of line to investigate a belt, a bookmark, or a mouse pad, but if the item is near enough to touch, a person might decide to purchase it and be less bored while waiting.

Application Exercise

Visit a retail establishment and see which of the shopper-friendly methods mentioned in the reading are being employed and which are being ignored. Spend at least an hour in the store watching consumer behavior. What do people touch? How do they respond to waiting in line? Be ready to report your findings to the class.

Predicting

For each set, write the definition on the line next to the word to which it belongs. If you are unsure, return to the reading on page 158, and underline any context clues you find. After you've made your predictions, check your answers against the Word List on page 163. Place a checkmark in the box next to each word whose definition you missed. These are the words you'll want to study closely.

Set One

takes away	to get	a customer	bumped or brushed against	tending to promote

☐ 1. **garner** (line 1) _____

☐ 2. **consumer** (line 2) _____

☐ 3. **detracts** (line 10) _____

☐ 4. **jostled** (line 12) _____

☐ 5. **conducive** (line 14) _____

Set Two

possible	a special right	advocates	shrewdness	to credit

☐ 6. **attribute** (line 18) _____

☐ 7. **proponents** (line 33) _____

☐ 8. **prerogative** (line 40) _____

☐ 9. **acumen** (line 57) _____

☐ 10. **feasible** (line 70) _____

Self-Tests

1 In each group, circle the word that does not have a connection to the other three words.

1. advocate	attacker	proponent	defender
2. consumer	shopper	producer	customer
3. push	shove	jostle	share
4. impossible	suitable	attainable	feasible
5. detract	divert	distract	promote
6. insight	shrewdness	stupidity	acumen
7. give	acquire	get	garner
8. right	privilege	prerogative	powerlessness
9. quality	attribute	characteristic	whole
10. helpful	worthless	conducive	useful

2 Finish the ad copy using the vocabulary words. Use each word once.

> **VOCABULARY LIST**
>
> | | | | | |
> |---|---|---|---|---|
> | feasible | acumen | detract | garner | attribute |
> | prerogative | conducive | proponent | jostle | consumer |

1. The smart _____ knows that to impress your guests you should serve a Gobbler Turkey for Thanksgiving.

2. It's a woman's _____ to change her mind, but you won't once you try Derriere Jeans.

3. A warm cup of Matthew's Cocoa—nothing is more _____ to a relaxing evening.

4. Making learning educational doesn't have to _____ from the fun. We combine education and fun at Kids Creative Software. Visit us today to see how.

5. _____ points with the kids by serving a cold pitcher of Paradise Lemonade today.

6. Family members _____ each other to be the first to read *Natural History Alive*; give your family a subscription today.

7. You didn't think a trip to Europe was _____ this summer. Think again! Quest Travel has tours for as little as $75 a day with all meals included.

8. You can _____ tomorrow's success to today's decisions. Northernmost College—an institution that helps you build a future.

9. Visit Smartalert.com for books on every subject. We've always been a(n) _____ of brighter minds.

10. Combining business _____ with understanding people. Invest with Quistex and watch your money grow.

3 Put yourself in the following situations, and match each situation to the word that applies.

Set One

1. You buy three shirts and two pair of pants. _____

2. At the City Council meeting, you argue in favor of preserving an open area as a park instead of building a shopping mall. _____

3. As guest of honor, you get to decide where to eat. _____

4. People at a party tell you that your kindness is one of your qualities they most admire. _____

5. You wear a beat-up hat with your tuxedo. _____

VOCABULARY LIST

proponent

detract

attribute

consumer

prerogative

Set Two

6. You contemplate whether you can attend a meeting at 6 p.m. and still make it to the movies with a friend at 8 p.m., twenty miles away. _____

7. You manage to get tickets to the sold-out concert. _____

8. You invest $150 in stocks, and by following the market, you end up with $1500 in one year. _____

9. You push your way through the crowd to the clearance rack. _____

10. You take a warm bath to help you go to sleep. _____

VOCABULARY LIST

garner

jostle

conducive

feasible

acumen

Word Wise

Collocations

Classical music can be *conducive to* a relaxing evening. (Chapter 26)

It is considered to be a *woman's prerogative* to change her mind. (Chapter 26)

If a store owner doesn't have much *business acumen,* he or she should hire someone to take charge of financial matters. (Chapter 26)

Word Pairs

Proponent/Opponent: A proponent (Chapter 26) is "one who argues in favor of something." An opponent is "one who is against something." The proponent argued for the benefits of an extended after school program. His opponent said the plan was too expensive.

Interesting Etymologies

Acumen (Chapter 26): comes from Latin *acumen,* "a point, sting," which has a root in *acuere,* "to sharpen." Acumen then means "keen insight; sharpness."

Interactive Exercise ||||||||||||||||||||||||||||||||||||||||||||||||||||||||||||||||||||

Put yourself in the consumer's frame of mind. Come up with a product, and write a sales pitch for it using at least five of the vocabulary words. Be creative; think about the types of products likely to generate interest among your friends and family.

_____

_____

_____

_____

_____

_____

_____

_____

_____

_____

_____

_____

_____

_____

Word Part Reminder

Below are a few short exercises to help you review the word parts you have been learning. Fill in the missing word part from the list, and circle the meaning of the word part found in each sentence. Try to complete the questions without returning to the Word Parts chapter. This Reminder focuses on roots from all three Word Parts chapters. Refer to the Word Parts list on the inside back cover to find the page number if you need to look back at any of the chapters.

| sta | duc | mut | rog |

1. When I was chosen to lead a lesson on similes, I decided the best way to con_____t the lesson was with a worksheet where people could create comparisons based on my starter ideas.

2. It was her birthday, so Nicky thought she had the right to ask for a special breakfast, but her mom didn't agree that it was her pre_____ative to start the day with a bowl of ice cream.

3. I can always count on Bob to stand up for me; he has been a con_____nt friend.

4. I love to see how ordinary animals, like cats and dogs, change in horror films as they become huge _____ant beasts.

162   CHAPTER 26   Business

Word List

acumen
[ə kyōō′ mən,
ak′ yə-]

n. a keen insight; sharpness;
shrewdness

attribute
[v. ə trib′ yōōt]
[n. a′ trə byōōt′]

v. 1. to regard as resulting from a
specified cause; to credit
2. to consider as a quality
of the person or thing
indicated

n. a quality or characteristic
belonging to a person or
thing

conducive
[kən dōō′ siv]

adj. tending to promote or assist

consumer
[kən sōō′ mər]

n. a customer; a shopper; one
who purchases or uses goods or
services

detract
[di trakt′]

v. 1. to take away a part
(usually followed by *from*)
2. to divert; to distract

feasible
[fe′ zə bəl]

adj. capable of being done;
possible; suitable

garner
[gär′ nər]

v. to acquire; to collect; to get

jostle
[jos′ əl]

v. 1. to bump or brush against
others; to push or shove
2. to contend with; to
compete

prerogative
[pri rog′ ə tiv]

n. a special right, power, or
privilege

proponent
[prə pō′ nənt]

n. one who argues in favor of
something; an advocate

Words to Watch |||||||||||||||||||||||||||||||||||||||||||||||||||||||||||||||||||||||||||||||||||||||||||

Which words would you like to practice with a bit more? Pick 3–5 words to study, and list them below.
Write the word and its definition, and compose your own sentence using the word correctly. This extra
practice could be the final touch to learning a word.

Word	Definition	Your Sentence
1. _____	_____	_____
_____	_____	_____
2. _____	_____	_____
_____	_____	_____
3. _____	_____	_____
_____	_____	_____
4. _____	_____	_____
_____	_____	_____
5. _____	_____	_____
_____	_____	_____

Chapter

27

Chemistry

From Ancient to Modern Times

Chemistry is a science that has had an influence on society from the ancient Egyptians to the modern day. Among the first chemical experiments were those done by **alchemists**. From 300 B.C. to about 1700 A.D.,
5 alchemists conducted various experiments. Two of their major goals were to change inexpensive metals such as lead into gold and to find the **elixir** of life, a drink they believed would lead to eternal life. They were not successful with either **endeavor**, but they did begin
10 the foundation of chemical experiments. They created symbols for various substances and developed methods of **distilling** and purifying various chemical compounds. Their experiments helped in discovering the essential qualities of some chemicals.

15   Today, chemistry is used in areas from law enforcement to health. Chemistry has been valuable in the field of **forensics** in **analyzing** samples of blood and hair from crime scenes, even for crimes that may have happened years ago. For example, in the 1960s a historian suspected foul play in Napoleon's death in 1821 on the island of St. Helena. Arrangements were made to **exhume** his body, and a hair sample was then taken. Because hair doesn't decay, scientists
20 were able to do chemical studies on it checking for **toxic** substances. **Traces** of arsenic were found in Napoleon's hair, which led to the possible conclusion that he was poisoned at the age of fifty-one. More recently prisoners have been freed after years in jail thanks to DNA testing that wasn't available at the time of their conviction. Chemists have also worked with law enforcement in other areas, such as developing lightweight bulletproof vests from plastics and creating chemical sprays like tear gas to bring
25 criminals out of hiding without having to shoot them.

Chemistry plays a vital role in health fields from diagnosing diseases to creating new medicines. Blood tests, which serve
30 as the basis of most physical exams, were invented by chemists, and the blood samples are studied in labs by chemists. Chemists have created medicines that treat everything from motion sickness and ulcers to heart
35 attacks and depression. One area of chemistry that has made surgery much less painful is the creation of pain killers. In the past people often drank alcohol to deaden the pain of

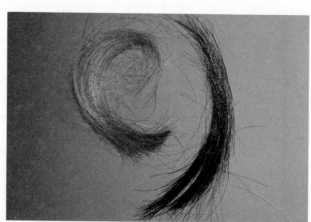

surgery, but chemists found ether to be a more effective pain killer. Later chemists developed local

40 anesthetics such as novocaine that can be applied to the area to be operated on, such as the mouth during dental work. Sometimes the discovery of a drug comes from a surprising place. In the early 1900s chemists were creating artificial dyes for cloth when Gerhard Domagk from Germany wondered if any of these dyes might work to destroy bacteria. At the time a bacterial infection could be fatal. In 1932 he tried a dye on mice that had serious bacterial infections. The mice were cured. He next tried

45 it on a little girl who had bacterial blood poisoning, and again it worked. Chemists continued Domagk's research to create other bacteria-fighting drugs. Chemistry also keeps us healthy by detecting **carcinogens** in food and food additives. Among the cancer-causing agents that chemists have discovered through experiments with lab animals were cyclamates (artificial sweeteners). After several years of testing, the Food and Drug Administration (FDA) banned cyclamates in 1970. Today

50 chemists are searching for better drugs to combat various cancers and AIDS.

Chemistry has a long history, is present in our everyday lives, and most certainly will provide future benefits. From the justice system to the kitchen table, chemistry continues to play an important role in the world.

Predicting

For each set, write the definition on the line next to the word to which it belongs. If you are unsure, return to the reading on page 164, and underline any context clues you find. After you've made your predictions, check your answers against the Word List on page 169. Place a checkmark in the box next to each word whose definition you missed. These are the words you'll want to study closely.

Set One

extracting elements	an attempt	medical knowledge used in law
people who practice a type of chemistry	a preparation believed capable of prolonging life	

❑ 1. **alchemists** (line 4) _____

❑ 2. **elixir** (line 7) _____

❑ 3. **endeavor** (line 9) _____

❑ 4. **distilling** (line 12) _____

❑ 5. **forensics** (line 16) _____

Set Two

cancer-producing substances	poisonous	examining	small amounts	to dig up

❑ 6. **analyzing** (line 16) _____

❑ 7. **exhume** (line 19) _____

❑ 8. **toxic** (line 20) _____

❑ 9. **traces** (line 20) _____

❑ 10. **carcinogens** (line 47) _____

1 Match the vocabulary word to the words you could associate with it.

_____ 1. elixir   a. crimes, techniques

_____ 2. distill   b. try, effort

_____ 3. forensics   c. deadly, lethal

_____ 4. toxic   d. dig up, uncover

_____ 5. carcinogen   e. gold, Middle Ages

_____ 6. alchemist   f. small, evidence

_____ 7. endeavor   g. separate, essential

_____ 8. analyze   h. prolong life, miraculous

_____ 9. exhume   i. cancer, substance

_____ 10. trace   j. study, examine

2 Finish the sentences. Use each word once.

VOCABULARY LIST

toxic	forensics	endeavor	elixir	distill
analyzed	trace	alchemist	exhume	carcinogens

1. Because Milt looks the same at 75 as he did at 25, his friends think he has discovered the _____ of life.

2. When we toured the _____ lab, we saw some of the equipment used to test blood and hair samples.

3. I was reading a mystery novel and was surprised by what could be combined with cologne to make a(n) _____ substance.

4. The family wanted to _____ Uncle Les when they thought he had been buried with Grandma Allison's hearing aid in his pocket.

5. The _____ worked late into the night trying different chemicals on the bar of lead, but it was still lead in the morning.

6. Scientists are still unsure of all the substances that are _____, but they range from overcooked meat to gasoline.

7. There wasn't a(n) _____ of evidence that Erik had been at the scene of the crime, but the police held him overnight anyway.

8. After doing the experiment, I _____ my lab report to see whether I could tell why I didn't get the expected result.

9. I will _____ to improve my grades by studying more every night.

10. Before the judge could make her decision, she had to _____ all the information the witnesses had given her.

3 Answer each question by writing the vocabulary word on the line next to the example it best fits. Use each word once.

VOCABULARY LIST

alchemist	carcinogen	elixir	exhume	toxic
analyze	distill	endeavor	forensics	trace

---

1. If Matthew says he will try to make it to your party, what will he do? _____

2. The police had to dig up the body after they suspected murder as the cause of death. What did they do to the body? _____

3. Gasoline has been labeled a cancer-causing substance. What is it? _____

4. A man set up a tent in town to sell a substance that he claimed could cure everything from arthritis to upset stomachs. What did he try to get the people to buy? _____

5. June decided she wanted to learn how to debate. What kind of class did she decide to take? _____

6. The gas that escaped from the factory made six of the workers seriously ill, and they were rushed to the hospital. What quality did the gas have? _____

7. In chemistry lab, Keri had to separate one chemical from another. How did she do this? _____

8. Simon, a young man who lived in the 1400s, experimented with chemicals to try to find a way to live forever. What was his occupation? _____

9. For her law class, Katy was given a court case and asked to study how the jury made its decision. What did she have to do to the case? _____

10. Karl is going to follow his family's journey from Sweden to America in the late 1800s. What is he going to do with his family's history? _____

Word Wise

Collocations

I will *endeavor to* find out what happened to Fluffy; I am sure she didn't just run away. (Chapter 27)

For centuries people have searched for the *elixir of life* without success. (Chapter 27)

Arsenic is a *toxic substance* that can be found in some water supplies. (Chapter 27)

Interesting Etymologies

Exhume (Chapter 27): comes from the Latin *ex-*, "out of," plus *humare*, "bury." *Humare* comes from *humus*, "earth." The meaning of exhume clearly comes from its roots: "to dig up something buried in the earth (especially a dead body)."

Interactive Exercise ||||||||||||||||||||||||||||||||||||||||||||||||||||||||||||||||||||

Notice how the vocabulary words are used in the background information and the Forensics Lab Report form below. Use as many of the vocabulary words as you can to complete the report.

Background Information: Mr. Harvey Watson's family has come to suspect murder in his sudden death. They have asked that his body be exhumed and analyzed for toxic substances. The day before Watson's death, he spent the morning working in his garden, and in the afternoon he spent several hours in his lab where he practiced alchemy. That night he ate a large dinner and drank heavily. Watson was fifty years old and had no known health problems. The family requests that every endeavor be made to distill the facts as to what could have caused Watson's untimely demise.

Forensics Lab Report

Examiner _____   Date _____

1. Name of the person exhumed: _____

2. Reason for the exhumation: _____

3. Substances and amounts of found in analyzing the body: _____

_____

4. Final analysis as to the cause of death: _____

_____

_____

Conversation Starters

An excellent way to review the vocabulary words and help to make them your own is to use them when you are speaking. Gather three to five friends or classmates, and use one or more of the conversation starters below. Before you begin talking, have each person write down six of the vocabulary words he or she will use during the conversation. Share your lists with each other to check that you did not all pick the same six words. Try to cover all of the words you want to study, whether you are reviewing one, two, or more chapters.

1. How would you describe your personality? Does your personality affect your education?

2. What types of art do you like? What attracts you to these styles? Do you dislike a type of art?

3. Which of the techniques in the Business reading have you seen applied in the places where you shop? Do you have a favorite place to shop? If so, what makes it so conducive for shopping?

4. How does chemistry play a role in your life? Would you drink an elixir of life?

Word List

alchemist
[al′ kə mist]

n. a person who practices alchemy (a type of chemistry popular in the Middle Ages)

analyze
[an′ ə līz′]

v. 1. to examine carefully
2. to separate a material into its basic parts

carcinogen
[kär sin′ ə jən′, -jen′]

n. any cancer-producing substance

distill
[dis til′]

v. 1. to extract the essential elements
2. to concentrate or separate by distillation

elixir
[i lik′ sər]

n. 1. an alchemic preparation believed capable of prolonging life indefinitely
2. a substance thought capable of curing all ills

endeavor
[en dev′ ər]

n. an attempt
v. to make an effort; to try

exhume
[ig zōōm′, eks hyōōm′]

v. to dig up something buried in the earth (especially a dead body)

forensics
[fə ren′ siks]

n. 1. a department of forensic medicine (the use of medical knowledge in civil or criminal law), as in a police laboratory
2. the study of formal debate

toxic
[tok′ sik]

adj. caused by a poison; poisonous

trace
[trās]

n. 1. an extremely small amount of a substance
2. evidence of some former action or event
v. to follow the history of; to discover

Words to Watch

Which words would you like to practice with a bit more? Pick 3–5 words to study, and list them below. Write the word and its definition, and compose your own sentence using the word correctly. This extra practice could be the final touch to learning a word.

Word	Definition	Your Sentence
1.		
2.		
3.		
4.		
5.		

28

Review

Focus on Chapters 24–27

The following activities give you a chance to interact some more with the vocabulary words you've been learning. By looking at art, taking tests, answering questions, doing a crossword puzzle, and working with others, you will see which words you know well and which you still need to work with.

Art

Match each picture below to one of the following vocabulary words. Use each word once.

VOCABULARY LIST

hues	relish	alchemist
exhume	portfolio	consumer

1. _____

2. _____

3. _____

4. _____

5. _____

6. _____

1 Pick the word that best completes each sentence.

1. _____ studies have shown that the initial results were correct: the drug's side effects can cause serious problems.

   a. tactile   b. toxic   c. subsequent   d. feasible

2. The kids enjoyed the _____ exhibit at the museum. They enjoyed touching the bones and skins of various animals.

   a. tactile   b. evocative   c. inherent   d. conducive

3. There are reports that you can cut down on the _____ in your meat if you sprinkle rosemary on your steaks or hamburgers when you barbeque.

   a. consumers   b. extroverts   c. portfolios   d. carcinogens

4. I realized too late that my partner's business _____ wasn't what he led me to believe. He finally revealed that we were seventy thousand dollars in debt, and we couldn't pay our employees any more.

   a. essence   b. acumen   c. introvert   d. elixir

5. I would _____ my math class this semester as one of the hardest courses I have ever taken.

   a. classify   b. jostle   c. endeavor   d. detract

2 Complete the following sentences using the vocabulary words. Use each word once.

a. distill	b. abstract	c. detract	d. eschews	e. jostled

1. I was determined that nothing was going to _____ from the beauty of my wedding day. I would simply have to ignore the thunder storm, nauseated maid of honor, and vivid orange tablecloths the caterer had brought by mistake.

2. The dentist said he would have to _____ one of my teeth. It was just too rotten to try to repair it.

3. The jockeys _____ each other as they headed toward the finish line; each one wanted to be in the best position for the final lap.

4. Trudy is the kind of person who _____ all conventional ideas. She even wore a swimsuit to a funeral.

5. I was able to _____ what the argument was about after I got reports from four different people who were present when it took place.

3 Finish the story using the vocabulary words. Use each word once.

Favorite Seasons

I have been trying to (1)_____ why fall is my favorite season. I (2)_____ my love of the fall to the colors. I am really fond of the warm oranges, yellows, and reds that for me are the (3)_____ of fall. There is also something about the harvest season that attracts me. Scenes of tables laden with turkeys, yams, rolls, and pumpkin pies are (4)_____ of home, family, and togetherness. The earth is so (5)_____ at this time of year that it makes me happy to see the abundant food we have to enjoy.

I also think that the fall appeals to me as a(n) (6)_____. The chill in the air allows me to sit by the fireside and chat with a friend or curl up alone under the blankets with a good book. Spring always seems to me more of a time for extroverts. People begin to leave their houses again. They go out to meet others just as the plants reach out to the sun and begin to bloom.

I tried to (7)_____ support for my personality and season theory from my friends. We ended up having a great time deciding which season fit each of us based on our (8)_____ traits. Colin is the most (9)_____ of the four of us, and he likes the fall the best. We decided that there is something in the changes that happen in the fall that call to a person's sensitive side. We were able to (10)_____ Amelia's love of summer to her sunny nature. She is easy to get along with just like a warm summer day is easy to take. Carlotta didn't think our system was very (11)_____, but I think she was just mad because we said her love of winter meant she was cold, though we were just joking. For now, I won't (12)_____ to go any further with my analysis of the seasons. I'll just take a walk and enjoy the gorgeous fall leaves.

Interactive Exercise ||||||||||||||||||||||||||||||||||||||||||||||||||||||||||||||||||||||||||||||||||||||

Answer the following questions to further test your understanding of the vocabulary words.

1. Name two conditions that are conducive to a good study session.

   _____   _____

2. Name three of your traits that make you a multifaceted person.

   _____   _____   _____

3. What is something that should be done sequentially?

   _____

4. If an elixir of life had been discovered by alchemists, who would you have wanted to take it so you could meet that person today? Why would you like to meet this person?

   _____

   _____

5. Do you consider yourself more of an introvert or extrovert? Why?

   _____

   _____

6. Who would you pay tribute to for encouraging your educational goals?

   _____

7. What is a perennial problem in either your life or in society?

   _____

8. In which area of forensics do you have more of an interest: medicine used in the law or formal debate? Why?

   _____

   _____

9. Name two toxic substances that should be kept away from children.

   _____   _____

10. What is something that is a teacher's prerogative? What is something that is a student's prerogative?

    _____

    _____

11. What are two items that you own that are emblematic of your interests?

    _____   _____

12. For what two ideas or causes are you a proponent?

    _____   _____

Crossword Puzzle

Use the following words to complete the crossword puzzle. You will use each word once.

VOCABULARY LIST

abstract	feasible
acumen	hue
alchemist	intuitive
analyze	multifaceted
attribute	perennial
conducive	portfolio
consumer	relish
elixir	subsequent
evocative	tactile
exhume	trace

Across

2. tried to turn lead into gold
7. Your plan is definitely possible.
10. perceptive
11. what an artist might carry
12. complex; to take out; a summary
18. continually recurring
20. following or coming after

Down

1. to dig up
3. He plays the piano, writes books, and builds houses.
4. to follow the history of
5. concrete
6. thought capable of providing eternal life
8. suggestive
9. to enjoy
13. buys groceries, clothes, and other items
14. examples: blue, purple, green
15. tending to promote or to assist
16. a keen insight
17. a quality belonging to a person
19. to examine carefully

HINT

Make Learning Fun and Meaningful

Think about the kinds of activities you like to do, and then try to incorporate the qualities involved in those activities into your learning experiences. If you like group activities (team sports, going to big parties), create study groups. If you like to draw, add visual elements to your notes, draw what happens in a story you read, or make a diagram to help you understand a concept. If you like to write, create stories or poems related to your studies or keep a journal about your learning. The more you enjoy what you do, whether in school or at work, the more you want to do it. Take the time to find ways to make your life and learning fun.

Mix It Up

Drama

Get together with some classmates to play charades. Use the words below or any of the vocabulary words you want to study. You can write the words on slips of paper and pick them out of a bowl or use your flash cards. One person picks a word, and the other people try to guess what word the person is acting out. You cannot use any words or sounds as you act out the word.

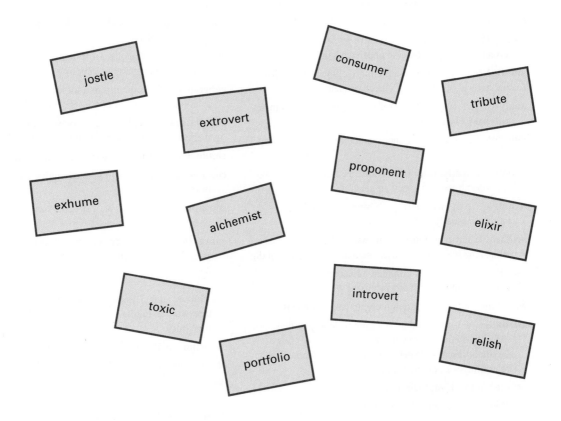

Glossary

A

abstract *adj.* 1. an idea not related to a specific example 2. not easily understood; complex *v.* 1. to take out; to extract 2. to summarize; to condense *n.* a summary

acoustics *n.* the features of a room or auditorium that determine the quality of the sounds in it

acrophobia *n.* a fear of heights

acumen *n.* a keen insight; sharpness; shrewdness

affluence *n.* 1. wealth; an abundance 2. a flowing toward

alchemist *n.* a person who practices alchemy (a type of chemistry popular in the Middle Ages)

alfresco *adv.* out-of-doors; in the open air *adj.* outdoor

alleviate *v.* to relieve; to reduce

ambiguous *adj.* 1. open to several possible meanings or interpretations 2. difficult to understand; unclear; indistinct

ambivalence *n.* having conflicting feelings, such as love and hate, about a person, object, or idea

analyze *v.* 1. to examine carefully 2. to separate a material into its basic parts

anecdote *n.* a short account of an interesting or amusing incident

annals *n.* yearly historical records, usually in chronological order; historical events in general

annotate *v.* to make notes or comments on or in the margins (usually in reference to a book)

artifact *n.* any object made by humans; a handmade object or the remains of one, such as found at an archeological dig

ascent *n.* 1. a rising or climbing movement 2. movement upward; advancement

ascertain *v.* to find out definitely; to learn with certainty

attribute *v.* 1. to regard as resulting from a specified cause; to credit 2. to consider as a quality of the person or thing indicated *n.* a quality or characteristic belonging to a person or thing

attune *v.* to adjust; to bring into harmony

audible *adj.* capable of being heard; loud enough to hear

autonomy *n.* independence; the quality of being self-governing

B

bon mot *n.* a witty remark or comment; witticism

bourgeoisie *n.* 1. in Marxist theory, the property-owning capitalist class 2. the middle class

burgeon *v.* to flourish; to grow; to sprout

C

cacophony *n.* a harsh, jarring sound

calculate *v.* to figure; to compute; to evaluate

carcinogen *n.* any cancer-producing substance

carpe diem *n.* seize the day; enjoy the present

censure *v.* to criticize in a harsh manner *n.* 1. a strong expression of disapproval 2. an official reprimand

cinematography *n.* the art or technique of motion picture photography

cite *v.* 1. to quote as an example or expert 2. to give as support or proof

clamor *v.* to state noisily *n.* a loud uproar; a loud and continued noise

classify *v.* 1. to organize; to categorize; to sort 2. to limit information to approved people

coherence *n.* the quality of a logical or orderly relationship of parts; consistency; unity

complacent *adj.* pleased with oneself, often to a dangerous degree; self-satisfied; untroubled

conducive *adj.* tending to promote or assist

connoisseur *n.* a person who can judge the best in an art or other field

consumer *n.* a customer; a shopper; one who purchases or uses good or services

conventional *adj.* 1. customary 2. conforming to established standards

D

deciduous *adj.* 1. shedding the leaves annually, as certain trees do 2. falling off at a particular stage of growth; transitory

decorum *n.* dignified conduct or appearance

derogatory *adj.* offensive; insulting; critical

descent *n.* 1. a downward slope 2. a decline; a fall; a drop

destitute *adj.* devoid; poor; impoverished

detract *v.* 1. to take away a part (usually followed by *from*) 2. to divert; to distract

deviate *v.* 1. to move away from a norm or set behavior 2. to cause to turn aside or to differ

diction *n.* 1. the choice and use of words in speech or writing 2. distinctness of speech

disconcerted *adj.* disturbed; disordered; confused

distill   *v.* 1. to extract the essential elements   2. to concentrate or separate by distillation

dolce vita   *n.* the good life (usually preceded by *la*)

doppelgänger   *n.* a ghostly double or counterpart of a living person

du jour   *adj.* 1. as prepared or served on a particular day   2. fashionable; current

E

elixir   *n.* 1. an alchemic preparation believed capable of prolonging life indefinitely   2. a substance thought capable of curing all ills

embed   *v.* 1. to fix deeply into something; to implant   2. to envelop or enclose

emblematic   *adj.* symbolic; representative

encrypt   *v.* 1. to put into a code   2. to change a file or e-mail message by using a code so it will be meaningless to unauthorized users if intercepted while traveling over a network

endeavor   *n.* an attempt   *v.* to make an effort; to try

epitomize   *v.* to serve as a typical or perfect example of; to typify

erosion   *n.* the process by which the surface of the earth is worn away by the action of water, winds, waves, etc.

escapade   *n.* an adventure, especially one contrary to usual or proper behavior

eschew   *v.* to avoid; to shun; to escape

essence   *n.* the quality of a thing that gives it its identity; the crucial element; core

evocative   *adj.* having the power to produce a reaction; suggestive

execution   *n.* 1. a style of performance; technical skill, as in music   2. the act of doing or performing   3. the use of capital punishment

exhume   *v.* to dig up something buried in the earth (especially a dead body)

expedition   *n.* 1. a journey made for a specific purpose, such as exploration   2. the group of persons occupied in such a journey

export   *v.* 1. to send overseas, especially items for trade or sale   2. to trigger the spread of in a different part of the world; to transmit   *n.* an item that is exported

extrovert   *n.* an outgoing person

F

fauna   *n.* the animals of a given region or period taken as a whole

faux pas   *n.* a mistake; a slip or blunder in manners or conduct; an embarrassing social error

feasible   *adj.* capable of being done; possible; suitable

flora   *n.* the plants of a given region or period taken as a whole

fluctuate   *v.* to vary irregularly; to change

foremost   *adj.* first in importance, place, or time; chief

forensics   *n.* 1. a department of forensic medicine (the use of medical knowledge in civil or criminal law), as in a police laboratory   2. the study of formal debate

fortitude   *n.* mental and emotional strength in bravely facing challenges or danger

G

gamut   *n.* the entire scale or range

garner   *v.* to acquire; to collect; to get

genre   *n.* a class of artistic work (movie, book, etc.) having a particular form, content, or technique; a style

H

hail   *v.* 1. to approve enthusiastically   2. to cheer; to welcome; to call out to

heinous   *adj.* wicked; vile; evil

hierarchy   *n.* a system of persons or things ranked one above the other

hinterland   *n.* back country; the remote or less developed parts of a country

horizontal   *adj.* 1. parallel to level ground   2. flat; at the same level

hue   *n.* color; tint; shade

humanoid   *adj.* resembling human beings; having human characteristics   *n.* a being with a human form; an android

I

imagery   *n.* the use of vivid descriptions to make mental pictures; mental images

immutable   *adj.* unchangeable

impervious   *adj.* 1. incapable of being injured, impaired, or influenced   2. not permitting passage

impromptu   *adj.* not rehearsed; spontaneous

inception   *n.* the act of beginning; a start

induce   *v.* to persuade; to cause

inference   *n.* the act of drawing a conclusion from evidence

inherent   *adj.* existing in someone or something as a permanent quality; innate

intention   *n.* a plan; an aim that guides action

intersect   *v.* to cross; to meet at a point; to cut through

introvert   *n.* a shy person

intuitive   *adj.* instinctive; perceptive; sensitive

J

jargon   *n.* 1. the language of a particular profession or group   2. unintelligible talk

jostle   *v.* 1. to bump or brush against others; to push or shove   2. to contend with; to compete

juxtaposition   *n.* an act of placing close together, especially for comparison or contrast

L

levity   *n.* 1. lightness of speech or manner; frivolity   2. lightness; buoyancy

levy   *v.* to impose or to collect, such as a tax

lichen   *n.* a complex organism composed of a fungus in symbiotic union with an alga, commonly forming patches on rocks and trees

M

magnanimous   *adj.* showing a noble spirit; unselfish; generous in forgiving

magnitude   *n.* greatness in significance, size, or rank

manifest   *v.* to reveal; to show plainly   *adj.* obvious; evident

martyrdom   *n.* 1. extreme suffering   2. the state of being a martyr (one who chooses death or makes a sacrifice rather than give up religious faith or other belief)

mean   *n.* the result found by dividing the sum of a set of numbers by the number of items in the set; the average   *adj.* holding a middle position

median   *n.* the middle number in a specified sequence of numbers (if the sequence has an even number of numbers, the average of the two middle numbers)   *adj.* relating to or located in the middle

metamorphosis   *n.* 1. a change in form from one stage to the next in the life of an organism   2. a transformation

metaphor   *n.* a figure of speech that makes a comparison between things that are not literally alike

meticulous   *adj.* 1. extremely careful and precise   2. excessively concerned with details

metrophobia   *n.* a fear of poetry

milieu   *n.* environment; surroundings

modulate   *v.* to alter (the voice) according to circumstances; to adjust

monolith   *n.* 1. a large single block of stone   2. a column or large statue formed from a single block of stone   3. something having a uniform, massive, or inflexible character

montage   *n.* 1. a film editing technique that presents images next to each other to convey an action, idea, or feeling   2. the combining of various elements to form a whole or single image

motif   *n.* the dominant theme in a literary or musical composition; a recurring element in a work of art

multifaceted   *adj.* many-sided; versatile; complex

multitude   *n.* 1. the quality of being numerous   2. a great, indefinite number   3. the masses

myriad   *adj.* of an indefinitely great number; innumerable   *n.* an immense number

N

nada   *n.* nothing

nomadic   *adj.* moving from place to place for survival; wandering; mobile

norm   *n.* a standard or pattern regarded as typical for a specific group

O

oasis   *n.* 1. a refuge, as from work or stress   2. a fertile area in a desert region, usually having a spring or well

ominous   *adj.* 1. threatening; menacing   2. pertaining to an evil omen

ostracize   *v.* to exclude, by general consent, from society or from privileges

oust   *v.* to remove; to force out

P

parallel   *adj.* 1. lines that go in the same direction and never meet   2. alike in some form   *n.* a likeness

paranoid   *adj.* showing unreasonable or abnormal distrust or suspicion   *n.* one afflicted with paranoia

paraphrase   *v.* to express in other words   *n.* a restatement of a passage using other words

parasitic   *adj.* pertaining to a parasite (1. an organism that lives on another species without aiding the host; 2. a person who takes advantage of others)

peninsula   *n.* an area of land almost fully surrounded by water except for a narrow strip of land connecting it with the mainland

perennial   *adj.* 1. lasting through the year or through many years; everlasting   2. continually recurring

permutation   *n.* alteration; transformation

persecute   *v.* to harass; to annoy continuously

personification   *n.* 1. the act of giving human qualities to ideas or inanimate objects   2. a person or thing that is the perfect example of a quality

pervasive   *adj.* having the quality to spread throughout; extensive

placate   *v.* to pacify; to calm

plagiarize   *v.* to use the words or ideas of someone else as one's own; to steal from another's writing

plateau   *n.* 1. a land area having a fairly level surface elevated above adjoining land; a tableland   2. a period with little or no change; a stable state

portfolio   *n.* 1. a portable case for holding loose sheets of paper or drawings   2. a list of the investments owned by a bank, investment organization, or other investor

posterity   *n.* 1. future generations   2. all of a person's descendants

posthumously   *adv.* 1. occurring after death   2. published after the death of the author

prerogative   *n.* a special right, power, or privilege

pristine   *adj.* unspoiled; pure; uncorrupted

procure   *v.* to obtain; to get by extra care or effort

proletariat   *n.* 1. in Marxist theory, the workers who do not own property and who must sell their labor to survive   2. the lowest or poorest class

prolific   *adj.* creating abundant works or results; plentiful; fertile

proponent   *n.* one who argues in favor of something; an advocate

Q

qualm   *n.* 1. a feeling of doubt or misgiving; uneasiness   2. a feeling of sickness, faintness, or nausea

quell   *v.* 1. to quiet; to pacify   2. to suppress

quota   *n.* 1. a part of a total amount; an allotment; an allowance   2. the number or percentage of people of a specified type allowed into a group

R

ramification *n.* 1. a development growing out of and often complicating a problem, plan, or statement; a consequence 2. the act of branching out

ravine *n.* a narrow, steep-sided valley, usually eroded by running water

refute *v.* to disprove; to show that a person or statement is wrong by argument or proof

relevant *adj.* pertinent; to the point

relish *v.* 1. to enjoy; to take pleasure in 2. to like the taste of *n.* pleasurable appreciation of anything; liking

repertoire *n.* 1. all the works that a performer is prepared to present 2. the skills used in a particular occupation

republic *n.* 1. a state where power rests with the citizens 2. a state where the head of government is usually an elected president

ritual *n.* 1. a set procedure for a religious or other ceremony 2. a custom; a routine *adj.* 1. ceremonial 2. customary; routine

S

sequential *adj.* characterized by a regular order of parts; in order; following

simile *n.* a figure of speech that compares two unlike things, introduced by the word *like* or *as*

socialization *n.* the process whereby an individual learns the values and behaviors appropriate to his or her culture and status

sojourn *n.* a temporary stay *v.* to stay temporarily

species *n.* organisms having some common qualities; kind or type

statistics *n.* 1. (used with a plural *v.*) data; numerical facts 2. (used with a singular *v.*) the science that deals with the study of numerical data

status *n.* 1. a relative position; standing, especially social standing 2. high standing 3. situation

stratification *n.* the act or process of developing levels of class or privilege

subsequent *adj.* following or coming after; succeeding

summation *n.* 1. a concluding statement containing a summary of principal points 2. the act of totaling; addition

surreal *adj.* unreal; fantastic; having the quality of a dream

symbiotic *adj.* 1. pertaining to the living together of two dissimilar organisms 2. any mutually dependent or beneficial relationship

symmetrical *adj.* regular in arrangement of matching parts; balanced

T

taboo *adj.* forbidden from use or mention *n.* a prohibition excluding something from use *v.* to forbid or prohibit

tactile *adj.* pertaining or perceptible to the sense of touch; concrete

telecommute *v.* to work from home by using a computer linked to one's company

terrain *n.* an area of land, especially in reference to its natural features

testimony *n.* evidence in support of a fact or assertion; proof

thesis *n.* a proposal that is defended by argument

totalitarian *adj.* 1. pertaining to a government that uses dictatorial control and forbids opposition 2. authoritarian *n.* an adherent of totalitarian principles or government

toxic *adj.* caused by a poison; poisonous

trace *n.* 1. an extremely small amount of a substance 2. evidence of some former action or event *v.* to follow the history of; to discover

tribute *n.* 1. something given or done to show one's admiration, appreciation, or respect 2. a payment or tax made by one nation to another for protection or to show submission

triumvirate *n.* 1. a government of three rulers or officials functioning jointly 2. any group of three

U

ubiquitous *adj.* existing or being everywhere, especially at the same time

underpinning *n.* a foundation or basis (often used in the plural)

utmost *n.* the greatest amount or level; maximum *adj.* most extreme; of the greatest degree

utopian *adj.* 1. resembling utopia, an ideal place 2. involving idealized perfection 3. given to impractical schemes of perfection

V

variable *n.* 1. a symbol that represents a changeable amount 2. something that may change *adj.* changeable; inconstant

venerate *v.* to regard with respect and reverence

verity *n.* 1. the quality of being real, accurate, or correct 2. a statement of principle considered to be permanent truth

viable *adj.* 1. practicable; possible 2. capable of living or developing

visualization *n.* the formation of a mental image or images

vivid *adj.* 1. clear; striking; dramatic 2. brilliant; having extremely bright colors 3. active; lively

voilà *interj.* There it is! (used to express success or satisfaction)

W

wane *v.* 1. to decrease; to decline 2. to approach an end *n.* a gradual declining

wary *adj.* cautious; watchful

Z

zeitgeist *n.* the spirit of the time; the general feeling of a particular period of time

Create Your Own Flash Cards

Using flash cards can be an immensely helpful way to study vocabulary words. The process of making the flash cards will aid you in remembering the meanings of the words. Index cards work well as flash cards, or make photocopies of the following flash card template to get you started. Put the word and the pronunciation on the front of the card. Elements you may want to include on the back of the card will vary according to the word and your preferred learning style. Consider the ideas below, and find what works best for you.

1. **The part of speech:** Write an abbreviation for the part of speech, such as *n.* for noun or *v.* for verb. This addition will help when you are writing sentences.
2. **A simple definition:** Use the definitions in the book or modify them to something that has meaning for you. Use a definition you can remember.
3. **A sentence:** Make up your own sentence that correctly uses the word. Try to use a context clue to help you remember the word. It might help to put yourself or friends in the sentences to personalize your use of the word. If you really like a sentence from the book, you can use that too.
4. **A drawing:** If you are a visual learner, try drawing the word. Some words especially lend themselves to this method. Your drawing doesn't have to be fancy; it should just help you remember the meaning of the word.
5. **A mnemonic (ni mon' ik) device:** These are methods to help your memory. They can be rhymes, formulas, or clues. For example: Stationery with an *e* is the kind that goes in an *envelope*. Make up any connections you can between the word and its meaning.
6. **Highlight word parts:** Circle one or more word parts (prefixes, roots, or suffixes) that appear in the word, and write the meaning(s) next to the word part: for example, induce. See the Word Parts chapters in the text for more on word parts.

    └─▶ *to lead*

Whatever you do, make the cards personally meaningful. Find the techniques that work for you, and use them in creating your cards. Then make the time to study the cards. Carry them with you, and study them any chance you get. Also, find someone who will be tough in quizzing you with the cards. Have the person hold up a card, and you give the meaning and use the word in a sentence. Don't quit until you are confident that you know what each word means.

Sample card

Front	Back
audible [ô′də bəl]	*adj. loud enough to hear* Even though she was whispering, Liz's comments were audible across the room.

Word List